Famous Brand Names and Their Origins

For Margaret and Gavin, two unique brands originating in the Thirties.

Famous Brand Names and Their Origins

Kathy Martin

PEN & SWORD
HISTORY

First published in Great Britain in 2016 by
Pen & Sword History
an imprint of
Pen & Sword Books Ltd
47 Church Street
Barnsley
South Yorkshire
S70 2AS

ISBN 978 1 78159 015 7

A CIP catalogue record for this book is available from the British Library

Typeset in Ehrhardt by
Mac Style Ltd, Bridlington, East Yorkshire
Printed and bound in India by Replika Press Pvt. Ltd.

Pen & Sword Books Ltd incorporates the imprints of Pen & Sword Archaeology,
Atlas, Aviation, Battleground, Discovery, Family History, History, Maritime,
Military, Naval, Politics, Railways, Select, Transport, True Crime, and Fiction,
Frontline Books, Leo Cooper, Praetorian Press, Seaforth Publishing and
Wharncliffe.

For a complete list of Pen & Sword titles please contact
PEN & SWORD BOOKS LIMITED
47 Church Street, Barnsley, South Yorkshire, S70 2AS, England
E-mail: enquiries@pen-and-sword.co.uk
Website: www.pen-and-sword.co.uk

Contents

Introduction

If the world sometimes seems to be changing with terrifying rapidity, surely there is a small measure of reassurance to be found in the knowledge that many of our most popular consumer brands have been with us for generations. In the supermarkets, in our homes, on the high street and in our leisure time we repeatedly come into contact with products bearing names that our forebears would recognise.

Imagine, if you will, a genteel lady from the late Victorian era finding herself transported by a time machine into the present. Bewildered by twenty-first century technology, astonished by our medical advances and very likely appalled by modern dress and behaviour, she may well require something to steady her nerves: a calming cup of Twinings tea, perhaps, or, should a stronger beverage be required, a restorative glass of Guinness. Since both brands were well-established in her day, their familiar presence might leave her sufficiently emboldened to catch up on world events. She could do this by glancing at a copy of *The Times*, already well-established in her own day or, for a lighter read, by perusing the latest issue of *The Lady* which was first published in 1885. Of course all the aforementioned products looked rather different in her era but the point is that our intrepid time traveller would recognise and be comforted by their brand names.

Conversely, the purpose of this book is to serve as a guide for those wishing to time travel in the opposite direction. Journeying into the past to look at some of the most popular consumer brands found in everyday life – tracing their origins, their development and their place in society today – we will discover that there is much more to celebrate than the simple fact of their continuing existence. Ingenious inventors, daring entrepreneurs, determined Nonconformists, spirited widows, gutsy refugees, forward-thinking philanthropists and a handful of decidedly racy characters; who knew the originators of our most famous brand names were so colourful?

What and where

For ease of navigation, the book is divided into two parts, Food & Drink and House & Home. In the first you will find chapters covering edible brands ranging from confectionery to beverages. And, since not everything we eat is branded, at the close of Food & Drink there is an extra chapter dealing with the origins of unbranded generic eponyms such as Beef Wellington and Waldorf Salad. In House & Home, meanwhile, you will find everything from toys and travel guides to Sellotape and supermarkets.

To set the scene, each chapter opens with an explanatory paragraph or two before moving on to the featured brands which are listed in alphabetical order. Additionally, for some brands, 'Did you know … ?' boxes have been included, containing snippets of information that may not be entirely relevant to the brand's story but are interesting nonetheless.

Getting down to the nitty gritty

With an almost infinite number of products to choose from, it was decided that to qualify for inclusion, brands had to meet the following conditions:

- they must be at least fifty years old
- remain in production today
- possess widespread consumer appeal

Furthermore, the decision was made to focus on brands with engaging or otherwise noteworthy histories. Fortunately, even after these criteria had been applied there were still rich pickings to choose from because, by and large, the pioneering entrepreneurs of yesteryear were a lively crowd.

Of course, some brand names remain well-loved long after they have fallen into extinction. In order to include at least a few of these 'fallen', each category features a 'gone but not forgotten' section. Similarly, brief 'honourable mentions' have been given to a number of popular brands that have not yet reached their half-century and therefore fail to qualify for full inclusion.

Now, gentle reader, with the thought processes behind this book duly explained, all that remains is for you to settle back and prepare for an enjoyable meander down memory lane. The wearing of rose-tinted spectacles is optional.

Part I

Food & Drink

Chapter 1

The Pantry

Prior to the invention of the refrigerator, perishable food items such as butter, cheese, milk, eggs and meat were stored inside small rooms or large cupboards known as pantries and larders. Located either inside the kitchen or adjacent to it, these rooms were usually north-facing to keep them out of the sun. Some had mesh-covered windows which allowed fresh air to circulate whilst keeping flies away. To help them stay cool, the perishable foodstuffs were placed on stone slabs although if space allowed joints of meat would be hung from ceiling hooks.

Did you know ...?

The word pantry is derived from '*pain*', the French word for bread which itself comes from '*panis*', the Latin word for bread.

Originally, when most people still created their meals from scratch using a few basic ingredients, the walls of the pantry or larder would be lined with shelves containing longer-lasting foodstuffs such as flour, sugar, salt and spices. It wasn't until the nineteenth century that the first convenience foods became available but thereafter the pantry shelves of a prosperous household groaned with a cornucopia of tempting products, all designed to make life easier for the busy cook.

Canned food had been available in Britain since 1813 but for much of the century it was mainly regarded as a useful tool for the armed forces and intrepid types such as polar explorers. It wasn't until the early years of the twentieth century that it really caught on with the public, perhaps because until then nobody had thought to invent a decent can opener. After that, however, canned food had arrived in a big way and its place on pantry shelves across the nation was assured.

Did you know …?

Napoleon is indirectly responsible for the invention of canned food. Keen to keep his troops well fed when they were far from home, he offered a reward to anyone able to devise a way of providing nutritious, long-lasting food. A confectioner called Nicholas Appert found that food heated in sealed glass jars would keep for a long time. Another Frenchman, Philippe de Girard, took the idea a step further when he used tinplated cans instead of the highly breakable glass jars. He sold his idea to an English merchant, Peter Durand, who promptly took out a patent to preserve food using the tinplated cans. Durand then sold the patent to an English entrepreneur called Bryan Donkin. In 1813 Donkin set up the first canned food factory, Donkin, Hall and Gamble, in Matlock, Derbyshire.

Thus it can be said that Napoleon is the godfather of canned foods, Appert the grandfather and Girard the father; Donkin, meanwhile, is the ingenious uncle who took the idea by the scruff of its neck and turned it into a viable commercial enterprise.

Ambrosia – dairy delights since 1917

While there may be other brands of tinned rice pudding on our supermarket shelves, to most people the product is synonymous with Ambrosia. The company was founded in 1917 in Lifton, a village located just inside Devon's border with Cornwall, by a local man called Albert Morris. Initially the Ambrosia creamery turned fresh locally-sourced milk into dried milk suitable for infants and invalids. Dried milk was also supplied to the troops fighting at the Front during the First World War. The milk was delivered daily to the creamery in vast churns and then dried with roller dryers.

Sometime during the 1930s – accounts vary as to precisely when – the creamery started to produce its tinned rice pudding which became an instant hit with the public. Still based in Lifton today, where it provides employment for around 270 people, Ambrosia continues to use milk sourced only from the south-west. In 1990 the company was sold to Colman's who in turn were acquired by Unilever in 2001. Since 2004, however, Ambrosia has been part of the Premier Foods family.

Did you know … ?

During the Second World War tins of Ambrosia Creamed Rice were placed inside Red Cross food parcels.

Baxters – more than a soupçon of quality since 1929

From relatively modest beginnings, Baxters have gone on to win worldwide fame and royal recognition, thanks in no small part to the skill and entrepreneurial flair of successive generations of their womenfolk. The story began in 1868 when 25-year-old George Baxter left a gardening job on the Gordon Castle Estate to open his own grocery shop in the village of Fochabers, located on the east bank of the River Spey, funded by a loan from his family. As a sideline, Baxter's wife Margaret made jams and jellies which were sold in the shop and found favour with his former employer, the Duke of Richmond and Gordon.

In 1916 the couple's son, William, built a factory on some land bought from the Duke. Continuing in the tradition of her mother-in-law, William Baxter's wife, Ethel, created an exceptional range of jams which William marketed throughout Scotland. Then, in 1923, Ethel hired a canning machine and began canning locally-grown fruit such as strawberries, raspberries and plums, in syrup.

In 1929 Ethel took the pivotal step of introducing soups to the Baxters range, utilising the wide range of excellent produce virtually on their doorstep. Products like Baxters Royal Game Soup soon acquired a following with the clientele of leading shops including Harrods and Fortnum & Mason. More flavours were introduced in 1952 when Ena Baxter joined the company; together with her husband Gordon she created a range of traditional Scottish soups that included Scotch Broth and Cock-a-leekie.

In the 1950s Baxter's were riding high; their soups were exported all over the world and the firm was awarded Royal Warrants by the Queen, the Queen Mother and King Gustav of Sweden. In 1992 another Baxter woman, Gordon Baxter's daughter Audrey, made her mark on the family business when she took over as Managing Director. She now insists on tasting every new recipe before the product can be approved.

As of 2015 Baxters remains a family business and although soup is now the firm's flagship product, accounting for about 70 per cent of its sales, it still produces a range of jams and condiments.

Bird's Custard Powder – under-egging the pud since the 1840s

We Brits have been pouring a sweet sauce made from Bird's Custard Powder on our puddings for over 160 years. Yet to purists, this undeniably toothsome product isn't custard at all because it doesn't contain egg and as the food experts know, you can't have true custard without egg.

Actually, that's the whole *raison d'être* behind Bird's Custard Powder. It was invented sometime in the 1840s by Birmingham chemist Alfred Bird who wanted his egg-allergic wife to be able to enjoy eating custard. Mrs Bird was very partial to the stuff but her digestion suffered when she gave in to her cravings. Her dilemma inspired Alfred to tinker about in his lab until he had come up with an egg-free alternative to custard. Not only did his cornflour-based creation please Mrs Bird, it also found favour with the British public when it went into mass production.

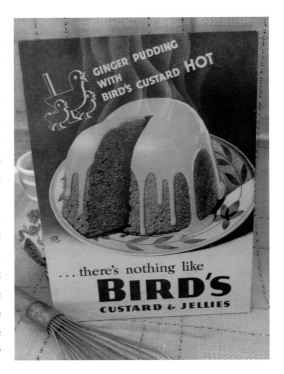

When Alfred died in 1879 his son, another Alfred, took control of the company, introducing new ranges such as blancmange and jelly. In 1922 Bird's rebranded with the red, yellow and blue packaging that is still used today. The three-bird logo appeared at the same time. Today Bird's is part of the Premier Foods group.

Did you know ... ?

We also have Mrs Bird's digestive problems to thank for the existence of Baking Powder; before tackling egg-free custard, her husband sought a solution to her yeast intolerance. He came up with Bird's Fermenting Powder which was later renamed Baking Powder.

Bisto – aboard the gravy train since 1908

'Ah! Bisto'. Roast dinner enthusiasts have been trotting out the famous gravy powder's catchphrase for more than ninety years while the product itself dates back to 1908. That was when Messrs Roberts and Patterson, employees of the Cerebos salt company, formulated a recipe for an easy-to-use gravy powder. According to legend, it was at their wives' request that they came up with the recipe; apparently the ladies were unable to make satisfactory gravy so they turned to their husbands for help.

Whether or not the story is apocryphal, an unfair slur on the culinary prowess of Mrs Roberts and Mrs Patterson, what is undeniable is that the resulting product made it much easier to create lump-free, flavoursome gravy. For that reason it rapidly found favour with the British public and in 1919 the brand's popularity received a further boost when the Bisto Kids first featured on Bisto's advertising and packaging.

Illustrator Will Owen created the pair of scruffy street urchins who sniffed the air appreciatively as they caught the appealing aroma of Bisto gravy, prompting them to utter the memorable 'Ah! Bisto' catchphrase. The hungry duo's rather wistful enthusiasm for Bisto resonated with the public to such an extent that they achieved cult-like status, especially during the Twenties and Thirties. The Bisto Kids remained a fixture on Bisto ads until 1996 when they were quietly dropped as part of the brand's efforts to appear more contemporary. However, the 'Ah! Bisto' slogan survives to this day.

The arrival of Bisto Granules in 1979 took gravy-making to a new level of simplicity; now, if you can boil a kettle you can make palatable gravy to accompany your sausage and mash. Today the brand is owned by Premier Foods.

Did you know ... ?

The Bisto name is an acronym of the phrase 'Browns Instantly, Seasons and Thickens in One'.

Bovril – beefing up Britain since 1886

The meat extract known as Bovril was created by a teetotal butcher from Edinburgh called John Lawson Johnston; he was born John Johnston but added the Lawson on his marriage to Elizabeth Lawson in 1871. Having studied chemistry for a while at Edinburgh University, Johnston conducted experiments in food preservation in his spare time and this pastime ultimately led to the development of a product which he named Johnston's Fluid Beef.

His big break came in 1874 when he was commissioned by the French government to look into the potential benefits of concentrated beef products. At the time the French were still smarting from the catastrophic pummelling their troops had taken in the Franco-Prussian War and they thought that improved nutrition might lead to a stronger army. Taking his family to Canada, Johnston opened a factory and began producing his Fluid Beef. The timing was serendipitous because a new Canadian law restricting the sale of alcohol had left the populace searching for a hearty, non-alcoholic substitute. Johnston returned to Britain in 1884, opening a factory in London for the manufacture of his unique product which was renamed Bovril in 1886. The name came from '*Bos*', the Latin word for ox, and '*Vril*', a word meaning energy force which was taken from *The Coming Race*, an 1870 novel by Edward Bulwer-Lytton.

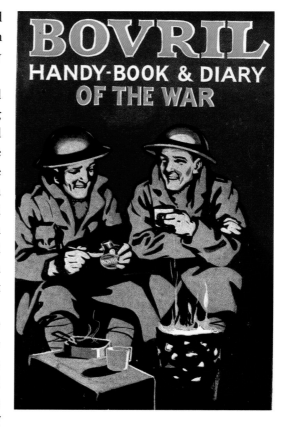

In 1893 Bovril began a sustained advertising campaign aimed at promoting the product's health benefits (Will Owen, the illustrator who created the Bisto Kids, produced many ads for the Bovril campaign). Its beneficial effect on Britain's armed forces was emphasised in advertising slogans used during both the Boer War and First World War, and it received glowing testimonials from such patriotic luminaries as Robert Baden-Powell and Rudyard Kipling.

Johnston sold Bovril to Ernest Hooley in 1896 for £2 million. The company was sold again in 1971, this time to Cavenham Foods, and it is now owned by Unilever. In 2004, in a bid to make it suitable for vegetarians, Bovril's beef content was dropped and replaced with savoury yeast. However, the change was short-lived and Bovril is beefy once more.

Did you know ... ?

Scottish-born Bovril-inventor John Lawson Johnston had a quick wit and a nice way with one-liners. When asked by a facetious journalist how, if Bovril was so indispensable, our forefathers had managed to survive without it, he replied without missing a beat: 'They didn't - they are all dead.'

Branston Pickle – bringing it out since 1922

Something of a British institution, Branston Pickle has been enlivening our cold cuts and sandwiches since 1922. Produced by Crosse and Blackwell, a food company established in the early nineteenth century, the pickle is made to a recipe said to have been developed by a Mrs Graham and her daughters, Evelyn and Ermentrude. Their combination of diced vegetables including cauliflower, carrot, swede, onion and gherkin mixed with a sweet vinegary sauce enhanced with spices excited British palates accustomed to blander fare. The original recipe remains unchanged today and is still a winner, with more than 17 million jars purchased every year. High-profile fans include Rolling Stone Keith Richards who allegedly takes it on tour with him, and fictional singleton Bridget Jones who eats hers straight from the jar.

Branston Pickle first went into production at Crosse and Blackwell's Branston factory – hence its name – near Burton upon Trent in Staffordshire. The site had been built during the First World War as a Government armaments factory but it was not completed until after hostilities had ceased. In 1921 Crosse and Blackwell purchased the site and relocated their pickle and preserves operation from London, employing 600 people, approximately two-thirds of whom were women. However, the move proved too costly for Crosse and Blackwell and by 1925 Branston Pickle was being produced in London's Bermondsey area. Thus the famous pickle's association with the village for which it was named proved somewhat short-lived. After Bermondsey, Branston Pickle moved to a number of different locations including Tay Wharf in London, Peterhead near Aberdeen and Glossop in Derbyshire before arriving at its present location, Bury St Edmunds in Suffolk.

The slogan 'Bring out the Branston' was launched as part of a nationwide advertising campaign in 1972. Intended to encourage consumers to use the jars of pickle lurking in their food cupboards, the catchy phrase caught the public imagination to such an extent that it is still closely associated with the product today even though it has not been used since 1985. In 1960 Crosse and Blackwell was bought by Nestlé who in turn sold the Crosse and Blackwell brands to Premier Foods in 2002. In October 2012 Premier Foods sold Branston Pickle to Japanese food empire Mizkan but production continues at Bury St Edmunds.

Did you know ... ?

A serious fire in 2004 at the Bury St Edmunds Branston Pickle factory precipitated fears of a nationwide pickle shortage. Premier Foods, owners of the brand at the time, ran full-page adverts in national newspapers reassuring concerned consumers that their favourite pickle would be available in time for post-Christmas turkey sandwiches.

Carnation Milk – milk to pour over since 1899

Many of us grew up pouring Carnation Evaporated Milk over our tinned fruit and today plenty of budding confectioners find Carnation Condensed Milk an indispensable aid to fudge-making. What few of Carnation's enthusiastic consumers know, however, is that the brand owes much of its long-lasting success to the innovations of a Swiss dairyman affectionately known as Cheese John.

Cheese John, real name John Meyenberg, worked for the Pacific Coast Condensed Milk Company (later renamed the Carnation Milk Company) which was established by Elbridge Amos Stuart at an existing factory located in King County, Washington, USA in 1899. The previous owners had been producing condensed milk – that is, milk which has been preserved by the addition of sugar – but when they went out of business Stuart took over the site. That was when Cheese John came up with the idea of sterilising the milk by subjecting it to high temperatures, thereby creating the first commercially-produced evaporated milk. Evaporated milk proved a real boon to

Did you know … ?

Carnation Milk acquired its name thanks to a tobacconist's window display. Company founder E. A. Stuart was thinking about a name for his new milk product when he spotted a cigar brand called Carnation. He thought it was a daft name for a cigar but apparently had no such reservations about applying it to tinned milk.

householders at a time when fresh milk wasn't always available or was unfit for human consumption.

Cheese John's usefulness didn't end there, as he also advised local dairymen about the best ways to produce the high yields of top-quality fresh milk that would be treated and turned into the evaporated product. Then, in 1910, the company established a farm which it stocked with prize Holsteins which went on to feature in Carnation's famous advertisements as 'contented cows'. In 1985 the Carnation brand was purchased by Nestlé.

Colman's Mustard – hot stuff since 1814

Mustard has been appreciated in Britain since Roman times. By the seventeenth century the condiment's punchy, powerful nature had led to the expression 'as keen as mustard' being used to describe characters who exhibited similar tendencies. History doesn't record if condiment king Jeremiah Colman was himself hot stuff but he certainly had a sound business brain, as evidenced by the fact that the mustard manufacturing enterprise he established in 1814 is still going strong 200 years later.

Colman was actually a flour miller when he acquired the existing mustard manufactory at Stoke Holy Cross, four miles south of Norwich. The business flourished and in 1823 Jeremiah took his oldest son, James, into partnership with him, forming the company J & J Colman. By 1851, the year Jeremiah died, Colman's had a workforce of around 200 people. In 1856 the business began relocating to its present site at Carrow Works in Norwich. The lengthy process was completed in 1862 and in 1866 the cheery yellow and red livery of Colman's Mustard first appeared on the product's label. That same year the company was awarded a Royal Warrant by Queen Victoria who clearly believed the condiment more than cut the mustard. Colman's retain the coveted Royal Warrant to this day.

In 1903 Colman's acquired a competitor, Keen & Sons of London, but contrary to popular belief this is not how the saying 'keen as mustard' originated; Keen's Mustard did not appear on the market until 1742 whereas the first recorded use of the saying was in 1672.

Another landmark in the company's history came in 1938 when Colman's merged with Reckitts of Hull, makers of many well-known household and pharmaceutical products. The new company was called Reckitts and Colman. In 1995, however, the Colman's part of the business was bought by food leviathan Unilever which continues to own it today.

Del Monte Canned Fruit – saying yes since the 1890s

The man from Del Monte says yes. That was the strapline for a long-running (and much-parodied) series of television ads revolving around an elegant man wearing a tropical suit and panama hat. The man from Del Monte was shown arriving at a fruit plantation where he would closely examine the crop while the workforce looked on apprehensively. When he signified his approval by saying 'yes' all would break into delighted smiles because it meant their fruit had been found good enough to satisfy Del Monte's stringent quality requirements.

Funnily enough, although the name Del Monte has long been synonymous with canned fruit and vegetables, the brand actually owes its origins to a coffee blend. Back in 1886 the Oakland Preserving Company in California developed a high-quality coffee blend for the Hotel Del Monte on the Monterey peninsula. A few years later when the California Fruit Canners Association (CFCA) was formed with the Oakland Preserving Company as one of the founding members, the Del Monte name was adopted as a label for the CFCA's premium products.

After a series of complicated mergers and consolidations, a major food conglomeration called Calpak emerged in 1916 and once again its premium brands were labelled Del Monte. The Great Depression brought hard times to Calpak but by the late 1940s the company was enjoying much greater prosperity thanks to the increased consumption of canned goods. In 1967 Calpak changed its name to Del Monte Corporation and some twelve years later it was acquired by RJR Nabisco. Since 2011, Del Monte Foods has been owned by an investor group led by KKR & Co. L.P.

Did you know … ?

Brian Jackson, the English actor who played 'the man from Del Monte' in the television ads, once starred opposite the legendary Ginger Rogers in the musical *Mame* at the Theatre Royal, Drury Lane.

Fray Bentos Pies – canning pies since 1961

It might intrigue aficionados of Fray Bentos pies to learn that the meaty products they enjoy are named after a small town in Uruguay in which they were first produced. The town's original name was Villa Independencia but it changed sometime after the establishment of a food company called Société de Fray Bentos Giebert & Cie.

The Fray Bentos story began as the result of a collaboration between two Germans, one a distinguished chemist called Justus von Liebig and an engineer called George Giebert. In 1840 Liebig had invented a concentrated beef extract which he was unable to produce commercially because of the prohibitive cost of European beef. Hearing about Liebig's dilemma, Giebert told him about the prodigious waste of cattle flesh occurring at that time in Uruguay and Argentina, as a result of the animals being slaughtered for their hides alone.

Together Liebig and Giebert founded a company in Fray Bentos and began producing Liebig's Extract of Meat, using every part of the animal apart from its moo. A few years later they branched out into corned beef production which they sold under the Fray Bentos label. About twenty-five years later a modified version of Liebig's Extract of Meat was marketed under a new name, OXO (see OXO entry).

Fray Bentos tinned meat pies were launched in 1961. Ownership of the Fray Bentos brand has changed several times over the years, most recently passing in 2011 from Premier Foods to Princes and then almost immediately from Princes to Baxters. In April 2013 production began at the Baxters plant in Fochabers, Scotland, having relocated from Long Sutton in Lincolnshire.

Did you know ... ?

Fray Bentos translates from Spanish into English as Friar Benedict. The Benedict in question is said to have been a reclusive hermit who once inhabited the area in which Fray Bentos pies were made.

HP Sauce – a bit on the side since 1895

The story of HP Sauce could be read as a salutary lesson to would-be entrepreneurs that creating a best-selling brand is no guarantee of wealth. Just ask Frederick Gibson Garton, the Nottinghamshire sauce manufacturer who settled a debt by giving away the recipes and rights to some sauces of his own devising including HP, Daddies and several lesser-known varieties.

The son of a licensed victualler, Fred Garton had been developing his sauces for a few years when it became obvious that one showed real promise. When the rumour reached him in 1895 that this sauce – a vinegary concoction of garlic, shallots, ground mace, tomato puree, cayenne pepper, ground ginger, raisins, flour and salt – had been used in the Houses of Parliament, Mr Garton decided to call it Garton's HP Sauce.

However, Garton's undoubted talent for sauces wasn't matched by sound business acumen because he had somehow managed to run up a debt of £150 with one of his suppliers, the Midlands Vinegar Company. It doesn't sound a huge amount but back in 1899 it was a significant sum of money, roughly the equivalent of £13,500 today according to one inflation calculator. One day in 1899 Edwin Samson Moore, the owner of the Midlands Vinegar Company, came knocking on Mr Garton's door. He was hoping to recoup his money but instead came away with a much more valuable asset, ownership of Garton's sauces.

With the HP brand under his belt, Moore set about turning his new acquisition into a household staple. His masterstroke was to put a picture of the Houses of Parliament onto every bottle, reinforcing the connection between the sauce and the seat of government. He also promoted it by travelling the country, dispensing free miniature bottles of HP Sauce from tiny wagons drawn by Shetland ponies. From such unlikely beginnings are iconic brands created.

In due course the Midland Vinegar Company was renamed HP Foods and other lines were introduced. The company was acquired by Imperial Foods in 1967 and thereafter changed ownership several times before being bought by American food colossus Heinz in 2005. A year later production of the famous British brand moved from Birmingham to Holland. Today HP Sauce is exported to around seventy countries worldwide and some 28 million bottles are consumed annually. As for poor old Fred Garton, according to an interview given by his son John to the *Nottingham Evening Post* in 1986, the sauce was banned from his house and he refused to have it mentioned in his presence.

Did you know … ?

John Betjeman immortalised HP Sauce in his 1958 poem, *Lake District*:

'I pledge her in non-alcoholic wine
And give the HP Sauce another shake.'

Heinz Baked Beans – a mealtime staple since 1901

If you were alive in the 1960s there's a good chance that you'll remember the famous Heinz Baked Beans advertising jingle which ran: 'A million housewives every day pick up a tin of beans and say Beanz Meanz Heinz'. Introduced in 1967, the advert's perky tune and idiosyncratic spelling swiftly caught on with the British public to the extent that many Sixties survivors can sing along with the jingle nearly forty years later. Today, according to the Heinz website, UK households are more reliant than ever on their baked beans with an annual consumption rate of more than 485 million cans.

Of course baked beans are not the only product to be marketed under the Heinz label. In fact, you could be forgiven for assuming that there are 57 different varieties since that's what it says on a can of baked beans but the truth is that Heinz are responsible for around 5,700 different food products. So what is the origin of the '57 varieties' strapline?

Company lore states that in 1896, founder Henry J. Heinz was on a train when he spotted a footwear firm's advertisement for twenty-one different types of shoe. Intrigued by the advert, he spent some time counting up the number of different products his own organisation offered and when he reached fifty-seven he wrongly thought he had counted them all. Thereafter 'Heinz 57 Varieties' appeared on Heinz products even though Henry had missed a few out from his initial tally.

The Heinz company was formed in the USA in 1876 by Henry J. Heinz, his brother John and a Heinz cousin called Frederick. Their first product was Heinz Tomato Ketchup which was introduced to the UK in 1886. Two years later Heinz opened an office in London and in 1901 the UK's first can of Heinz Baked Beans was sold by Fortnum and Mason. The combination of ready-cooked beans in a tasty tomato sauce found favour with the British public and in due course achieved the status of a store cupboard essential. Henry J. Heinz died in 1919, just a few years before his company opened its first production operation in the UK.

Did you know … ?

Every standard-sized can of Heinz Baked Beans contains an average of 475 beans.

Homepride Flour – graded grains since 1963

Although Homepride Flour has only been around for just over fifty years, the brand's origins can be traced back to 1897. That was when Spillers and Nephew of South Wales first started making and marketing pre-packed plain flour. (Self-raising flour did not appear until 1949 when a Bristol man called Henry Jones had the brilliant idea of adding raising agents to the plain variety).

In the Twenties a Midlands firm called Robbins and Power introduced a rival flour called Homepride. Spillers subsequently acquired Homepride but for a time they sat on the brand while they concentrated on their regional pre-packed flour brands. Then, in 1963 a technological breakthrough in milling processes meant that Spillers could offer a much better quality of flour with uniform granulation and no dust. They decided to launch their new improved flour nationwide under the Homepride label.

Two years later, American ad men Bob Geers and Bob Gross created the now iconic Fred the flourgrader character for a new Homepride advertising campaign. Fred is still very much visible today on Homepride's packaging and marketing and there is a thriving trade in vintage Fred collectables on the secondary market. The brand is currently owned by Premier Foods.

Did you know … ?

Fred the flourgrader - catchphrase 'Because graded grains make finer flour' - was voiced by English actor John Le Mesurier until his death in 1983. Le Mesurier enjoyed a long and successful acting career but is perhaps best remembered today for his portrayal of Sgt Wilson in the BBC's much-loved Home Guard sitcom *Dad's Army*.

Hovis – our daily bread since 1890

The Hovis story began in 1886 when Staffordshire flour miller Richard Smith developed a method for preserving the wheatgerm in bread. At first he called his new product Smith's Patent Germ Bread, launching a nationwide competition in 1890 to

The little golden heart of the wheat—
that's the wheatgerm. It's tiny but
packed full of natural goodness.
Lots of bread has none, Hovis has lots extra.

Hovis

the golden heart of the meal

Hovis toasted and buttered for dunking and munching all eggy and yolky. Hovis with kippers oak-smoked for breakfast, Hovis with wild heather honey. Hovis for eating with spicy cold bacon and chicken and cheese. Hovis and Hovis and Hovis because you simply can't beat it.

don't say brown—say **Hovis**

come up with a catchier name. Hovis, the winning entry, was supplied by an Oxford schoolmaster called Herbert Grime. It is derived from the Latin phrase '*hominis vis*' which roughly translates as 'strength of man'.

By 1895 over one million loaves of Hovis were sold every week. Marketed as a bread for the health conscious (Queen Victoria was said to be a fan), it was available in various sizes including 1lb and 2lb loaves, 8 oz. junior loaves and even tiny penny loaves.

Richard Smith died in 1900 but his bread business continued to flourish throughout the twentieth century, helped in no small way by the advertising slogan 'Don't say brown, say Hovis', which was launched in 1925. In 1957 Hovis merged with flour manufacturers McDougall to form a new enterprise called Hovis McDougall. Five years later another merger saw the inception of food giant Rank Hovis McDougall, known today simply as RHM. Since 2007 Hovis has been part of the Premier Foods group.

Did you know ... ?

Launched in 1973, the famous Hovis television commercial featuring a delivery boy struggling up a steep hill with his bicycle was made by Ridley Scott. Filmed on Gold Hill in Shaftesbury, Dorset, the commercial memorably featured music from Dvorak's New World Symphony. Scott, of course, went on to achieve worldwide fame as the director of a string of successful, critically acclaimed films including *Alien*, *Blade Runner*, *Thelma and Louise*, *Gladiator* and *Black Hawk Down*.

Huntley & Palmers – taking the biscuit since 1846

For over 150 years Huntley & Palmers were synonymous with biscuits, just as the company's hometown, Reading, was known throughout the world as 'Biscuit Town'. However, after a long and mutually prosperous association with the town, production in Reading ended in 1976 and within a couple of decades the Huntley & Palmers brand had fallen into abeyance. Happily, the name was resuscitated in 2004 and although production now takes place in Sudbury in Suffolk, it is good to know that Huntley & Palmers biscuits are once again available for afternoon tea.

Jacob's Cream Crackers – completely crackers since 1885

The Jacob's story began in 1850 when William Jacob, a Quaker, opened a small bakery in Waterford in the south of Ireland. Two years later Jacob had started producing biscuits on a larger scale in Dublin. However, it is thought that the recipe for the famous Jacob's Cream Cracker was dreamed up by one Joseph Haughton after a spot of experimentation in his home kitchen. Haughton's creation was introduced into the Jacob's range in 1885 where it has remained ever since. A second factory was opened at Aintree in Liverpool in 1914; it still produces biscuits today.

In 1960 Jacob's became W & R Jacob's & Co. After a few more name changes, they became part of the United Biscuits family.

> **Did you know … ?**
>
> There is no cream in a Jacob's Cream Cracker. The word 'cream' refers to part of the production process, the creaming together of flour, oil, salt and yeast, rather than an ingredient.

Kellogg's Corn Flakes – breakfast in a bowl since 1906

A bowl of cornflakes and a cup of coffee – for many people across the globe, that's the very definition of a good start to the morning. So it comes as something of a surprise to discover that this breakfast staple was apparently created by fluke. It happened in 1898 when Will Keith (W. K.) Kellogg and his brother, Dr John Harvey Kellogg, were attempting to make granola. Whilst experimenting, they accidentally flaked wheat and from this moved on to corn, eventually ending up with their recipe for cornflakes.

In 1906 W. K. Kellogg, a Seventh-day Adventist and vegetarian, opened the Battle Creek Toasted Corn Company in Battle Creek, Michigan. His intention was to provide Americans with an alternative to their heavily meat-based breakfasts. In 1915 Bran Flakes were added to the product range, with All-Bran appearing a year later. By 1922 the brand had arrived in the UK and today it can be purchased in 180 countries worldwide.

Cornelius Rooster, the perky green, red and yellow cockerel now found on all packets of Kellogg's Corn Flakes, made his debut in 1957. Kellogg's describe Cornelius as a symbol of waking up and getting the morning off to a good start but in Wales a different explanation is offered for his status as the cereal's special 'spokes-character'. According to a much-repeated tale, the company decided to adopt a cockerel mascot when Welsh harpist Nansi Richards told them that the name Kellogg was similar to *ceiliog*, the Welsh word for cockerel.

Did you know ... ?

During the Second World War, Kellogg's Corn Flakes were replaced in Britain by Kellogg's Wheat Flakes and Wheat Krispies which were produced from home-grown wheat.

Lyle's Golden Syrup – the sweet taste of success since 1881

Quite aside from being the archetypal store cupboard staple, Lyle's Golden Syrup has the distinction of holding the Guinness World Record for the world's oldest unchanged brand packaging. The superbly sticky product has been supplied in the familiar green and gold tin since 1883, apart from an unavoidable hiatus during the First World War when all available metal was required for the war effort.

The golden syrup story began in 1881 when successful Scottish entrepreneur Abram Lyle established a sugar refinery in East London, a short hop from the rival refinery owned by Henry Tate. Lyle soon realised that there was a market for 'Goldie', the name he gave the rich amber syrup produced during the refining process. Perhaps due to his early years in cooperage, he initially sold the syrup from wooden casks but switched to tins when demand began to grow.

Almost as famous as the green and gold tin is the product's unusual logo which depicts bees swarming around a dead lion. Appearing beneath the image are the words 'Out of the strong came forth sweetness' which are taken from an Old Testament quotation (Judges 14:14) known as Samson's riddle. Nobody seems to know precisely why it appears on a tin of syrup apart from the fact that Lyle was a deeply religious man.

In 1922, a year after Tate and Lyle merged their refineries to form a sugar behemoth, Lyle's Golden Syrup received the ultimate accolade of a Royal Warrant which it retains

Did you know ... ?

Captain Scott included a supply of Lyle's Golden Syrup when he set out on his doomed Antarctic expedition in 1910. When his provisions were rediscovered in 1956, the tin and its contents were found to be in good condition.

to this day. And it's not just the royals who love it; every month more than one million tins leave the Thames-side refinery and find their way into homes as far flung as North America, China, South Africa and Australia.

Marmite – extracting the yeast since 1902

While it may not be true that the world is divided into those that love or hate Marmite, there is little doubt that the distinctive taste of the savoury black spread inspires like and loathing in equal measure. Although it has many culinary uses, true fans know that little can beat the sublime pleasure of Marmite spread on hot, buttered toast.

Marmite is a yeast extract which originated as a by-product of the brewing industry. The Marmite Food Extract Company was established in Burton upon Trent in 1902, thanks to a much earlier discovery by German chemist Justus von Liebig (of Fray Bentos fame), that brewers' yeast – a commodity available in large supply in Burton thanks to the proximity of the Bass brewery – could be transformed into a tasty food product. In the early years of Marmite production demand for the product was low until people became aware of the dietary importance of vitamins. Marmite, it transpired, was chock full of health-inducing B vitamins. Once that was understood, the popularity of Marmite skyrocketed to the extent that during both World Wars, British housewives were exhorted to use it sparingly to leave enough to send to the troops fighting in far-off climes.

Marmite is still produced in Burton upon Trent although these days it is part of the Unilever group.

Did you know...?

The Marmite name is thought to derive from a type of covered French cooking pot, although the word also refers to a soup. Thus it would be possible to consume marmite cooked in a marmite with a side serving of Marmite on toast.

Nescafé – coffee on demand since 1938

It's a curious fact that Nescafé came into existence as a consequence of the 1929 Wall Street Crash. Coffee prices collapsed in the ensuing economic chaos, leaving vast quantities sitting unsold in a Brazilian warehouse. That was when Nestlé, the Swiss food company founded in 1867, was asked to find a way to transform the raw product into some kind of instantly soluble coffee whilst retaining its fresh aroma.

After a great deal of research and several false starts, a soluble coffee product called Nescafé made its debut in Switzerland in April 1938. Two months later it was introduced to the UK and the following year it arrived in the US where it proved immensely popular because of its long shelf life.

Not content to sit on their laurels, Nestlé continued to make improvements. In the 1960s tins were replaced with glass jars to enhance freshness and in 1965 a freeze-dried soluble coffee called Nescafé Gold Blend was introduced. Consumers of a certain age will remember the series of television commercials starring Anthony Head and Sharon Maughan which were first broadcast in the 1980s. Viewers became so absorbed by the couple's tentative romance that tabloid headlines were made when they finally exchanged a kiss after six years of indecisiveness.

There's always time for **NESCAFÉ**

Now Mother is converted to the quick way of making coffee by using Nescafé. She appreciates its roaster-fresh fragrance and enjoys its carefully blended flavour. Now *she* will rely on Nescafé—a spoonful in the cup, and near-boiling water added. The surest way of making really good coffee every time.

Nescafé is a soluble coffee product composed of coffee solids, combined and powdered with dextrins, maltose and dextrose added to protect the flavour

ANOTHER OF NESTLÉ'S GOOD THINGS

Ovaltine – bedtime in a mug since 1909

Virtually a byword for nostalgic cosiness, Ovaltine was developed in 1904 by Swiss chemist George Wander. Whilst studying barley malt, Dr Wander discovered that it is an excellent source of complex carbohydrates and vitamins. It then occurred to the good doctor to create a fortifying drink by combining the barley malt with milk, eggs and cocoa. In Switzerland his product is known as Ovomaltine, a name devised by combining *ovum*, the Latin for egg, with malt (which is spelled the same in French as

it is in English). When Ovomaltine was introduced to
the UK in 1909 it was launched as Ovaltine, according
to some reports as a result of a mistake on a trademark
application. Whatever the truth of the matter, a long
and happy association with the British public had just
begun.

Almost from the beginning, the marketing bods at
Ovaltine made use of clever advertising gimmicks to
promote their brand. In 1920s, they introduced the
Ovaltine Dairy Maid to emphasise the wholesome
nature of the drink. This success was followed in
1935 by the introduction of the League of Ovaltineys,
a free-to-join children's club complete with radio
show and catchy theme song. So popular was the
League that by 1939 it boasted more than five million
members.

Ovaltine was produced in Kings Langley, Hertfordshire, from 1913 until 2002 when
the brand was purchased by Associated British Foods. Today production takes place in
Switzerland, China and Thailand and it is marketed in fifty-four countries worldwide.

Did you know…?

In 1953 Sir Edmund Hilary kept warm whilst climbing Mount Everest by drinking
Ovaltine.

OXO – cooking with cubes since 1910

The origins of the OXO brand are rooted in the Fray Bentos story outlined earlier
in this chapter. In order to finance further growth in Uruguay, in 1865 Liebig and
Giebert launched a new enterprise, Liebig's Extract of Meat Company, in London.
Their product quickly won the approval of leading medical experts including no less
a luminary than Florence Nightingale. Evidently such endorsement proved effective
because *New York Herald* correspondent Henry Morton Stanley made sure to pack a
supply of Liebig's when he went to Africa in search of Dr David Livingstone.

Inevitably, the success of Liebig's Extract of Meat inspired others to produce similar
products and by the 1890s the company found itself hard pressed by competitors. Their
solution was to introduce a more affordable product which they launched in 1899. They

called it OXO and it was a runaway success, thanks in large part to Charles Gunther, the company's brilliant young marketing guru. He implemented an aggressive marketing strategy that for the time was remarkably modern, organising leaflet distribution, initiating gift programmes and engaging in a deluge of press and billboard advertising. Perhaps his most farsighted coup at this time was securing the position of official caterer to the 1908 London Olympics, ensuring his product was placed before the world's press in a way that indelibly linked it to health and fitness.

In 1910 OXO introduced their famous cube, just in time for it to be included in ration kits supplied to soldiers in the First World War. Another pivotal year in OXO's history was 1958 when 'Katie' showed viewers how to enhance their meals with OXO in the product's first TV commercials. From 1983 to 1999 the role of Katie was played by the late Lynda Bellingham. Today the OXO brand is owned by Premier Foods.

PG Tips – anytime cuppas since 1930

The PG Tips story started in 1869 when Arthur Brooke began retailing tea, coffee and sugar in Manchester, having learned about the tea trade while helping in his father's wholesale business. He named his shop Brooke, Bond and Company; Mr Bond did not exist but Brooke thought the name added a certain gravitas to his fledgling enterprise. At this time he coined the following slogan: 'Good tea unites good company, exhilarates the spirits, banishes restraint from conversation and promotes the happiest purposes of social intercourse.' As a slogan it may be a bit wordy but it's memorable all the same, if only for giving tea the inhibition-busting properties more commonly associated with alcohol.

After opening shops in Liverpool, Leeds and Bradford, Brooke moved to London in 1872, setting up his company headquarters in Whitechapel. Initially it seemed he had bitten off more than he could chew but ultimately the enterprise prospered and when Brooke died in 1918 he was a wealthy man. However, it wasn't until 1930 that

PG Tips, the jewel in Brooke Bond's crown, was created. Originally the tea was called Pre-Gest-Tee because with its introduction the company was promoting the novel idea that tea could be consumed before eating; previously it had been very much regarded as a digestive. When retailers abbreviated the name to PG, the company suffixed it with 'tips' to underline the message that the tea is made from the top two leaves and bud of the tea plant.

In 1956 the first PG Tips television commercial was broadcast, starring four chimpanzees enjoying a chimps' tea party, and from that moment onwards the brand would be irrevocably associated with all things primate. The chimps were retired in 2002 but their adverts are still fondly remembered, especially the one featuring Mr Shifter ('Dad, do you know the piano's on my foot?'; 'You hum it, son, I'll play it!') and the Tour de France ('Avez vous un cuppa?').

At the time of writing the PG Tips commercials feature Johnny Vegas and his friend Monkey, voiced by Ben Miller. The brand is owned by Unilever.

Did you know … ?

The tea bag was invented by accident in 1908 when New York tea merchant Thomas Sullivan mailed customers samples of tea contained in small silk bags. Not realising that they were first meant to remove the tea from the bag, some popped the whole thing into a teapot and thus the tea bag was born, although it wasn't until 1953 that Tetley were bold enough to introduce it to British tea drinkers.

Shredded Wheat – breakfast biscuits since 1892

When Henry Perky of Denver, Colorado, invented his boiled wheat biscuit in 1892, he was hoping to market the machine used to form the biscuit rather the foodstuff itself. For that reason he gave his company the unambiguous name of The Cereal Machine Company. However, Perky had a rethink when he realised that people were more interested in the cereal biscuits than his machines. Undeterred, he relocated to New England where he opened a bakery called The Shredded Wheat Company. In 1901 he moved again, this time to Niagara Falls where he established the so-called Palace of Light, a modern, clean work environment well ahead of its time in terms of employee well-being. After a brief flirtation with yet another company name, in 1908 Perky settled once and for all on The Shredded Wheat Company.

As part of a programme of expansion, in 1925 a Shredded Wheat plant was opened in the UK in Welwyn Garden City. Three years later the company was sold to The

National Biscuit Company which ultimately changed its name to Nabisco. After changing ownership a number of times, the English operation is now run by Cereal Partners-UK, a General Mills–Nestlé consortium.

Twinings – top-notch tea since 1706

A London weaver by trade, Thomas Twining was a young man with a nose for opportunities. Specifically, he recognised the possibilities presented by tea, a new commodity introduced to the English in 1662 by Catherine of Braganza, Charles II's Portuguese consort. Initially tea was taxed so heavily, only the elite could afford to drink it. But far-sighted Thomas was so sure the commodity had potential that in 1701 he abandoned his loom in order to learn from an East India Company merchant who dealt in tea. Five years later, feeling confident enough to strike out on his own, he purchased Tom's Coffee House on the Strand.

Conveniently positioned for both Westminster and the City, the coffee house attracted an influential clientele, many of whom were wealthy enough to sample the high quality tea that Thomas began to offer alongside his coffee. It became quite the fashion for gentlemen to drink tea at Tom's Coffee House, although the aristocratic ladies were denied this pleasure as coffee houses traditionally were male-only preserves. Their response was to shrug their silk-clad shoulders and despatch their footmen to buy the loose tea for consumption at home.

Even though tea remained expensive, it continued to grow in popularity. Within a decade or so, Twining was able to convert three adjacent houses in the Strand into the world's first dry tea and coffee shop. It still exists today and, moreover, ten generations of the Twining family have worked in the business established by their ancestor.

Did you know ... ?

In 1837, long after Thomas Twining's demise, Queen Victoria awarded the company the coveted Royal Warrant and since then they have supplied every British monarch with tea. A special blend is produced for our current Queen but its specifics are a closely-guarded secret.

Gone but not forgotten: Bird's Instant Whip
Introduced in 1955, this miraculous dessert was ready to eat minutes after the addition of cold milk. Nutritionally-speaking, it probably wasn't the greatest but children loved it. It disappeared from supermarket shelves in the early years of the twenty-first century.

Honourable mention #1: Cadbury's Smash
Cadbury's launched Smash, the instant mashed potato brand, in 1969 although the famous Martians television advert was not aired until 1973. Smash is now owned by Premier Foods.

Did you know ... ?

In 1999 the Smash Martians advert was voted TV Ad of the Century by Campaign Magazine.

Honourable mention #2: Mr Kipling
Shock news: Mr Kipling, maker of 'exceedingly good cakes', was not a real person. Launched in 1967 by Rank Hovis McDougall, the Mr Kipling brand name was intended to lend a cosy aura to cakes turned out on a production line. It was a highly successful strategy because Mr Kipling has been the UK's leading cake brand since 1976.

Chapter 2

Thirst Quenchers: Alcoholic and Non-Alcoholic

The British may be known as a nation of tea drinkers but we're no slouches when it comes to cold beverages, either. In fact, every time we go shopping we are faced with a veritable ocean of branded drinks to choose from including fizzy pops, fruit-flavoured squashes, spirit, liqueurs, wines, beers and mixers. With new products appearing on the shelves all the time it is inevitable that some acquire a faddish following, blazing brightly for a while before slipping into gentle obscurity. Others, however, have discovered the elusive formula that allows them to last the course. It is to these, then, that we raise a metaphorical glass and say 'Cheers!' as we look back on their origins.

Babycham – lovely bubbly since 1953

'I'd love a Babycham!' Simple yet memorable, it's a brand slogan that proved so effective that for a period during the mid-Fifties, supplies had to be rationed. Since then the sparkling perry tipple has drifted in and out of fashion but even during its leanest years it has retained the loyalty of a largely female customer base which has been drinking little else since it first appeared on the market in 1953.

The drink was created by Francis Showering, one of four sons from a small-scale brewing family based in Shepton Mallet in Somerset. Keeping afloat in a market increasingly dominated by the large breweries proved tricky for the Showerings but Francis was determined to succeed. Shortly after the Second World War he began experimenting with the perry pears widely grown in Somerset. By 1950 he had developed a sparkling alcoholic drink made from pear juice which he put in baby-sized bottles and entered into major agricultural shows. At this point the drink was called Champagne de Poire but when it proceeded to win first prize at every show it began to be known as the 'Baby Champ'.

In 1953 Showering was ready to launch his product nationwide. Now named Babycham, it was pitched as the perfect drink for women to choose on a night out. All the advertising was slanted towards the female market, from the appealing, Bambi-esque deer motif to the images of glamorous women sipping Babycham from champagne-style glasses. During the Sixties the enormous success of his creation enabled Showering to acquire well-known drinks companies such as Britvic and Harveys of Bristol, and to merge with Allied Breweries in 1968.

Francis Showering was awarded the CBE in 1982, as much in recognition for his work in West Country agriculture as for his success in business. He died in 1995 at the age of 83. Babycham, meanwhile, fell from favour during the Nineties when it was considered a little old-fashioned. However, it has recently experienced a recovery, perhaps occasioned by the upsurge of interest in all things mid-century retro. Although the brand is owned today by Accolade Wines, a global wine company based in Australia, it is still produced in Shepton Mallet.

Did you know … ?

In the Sixties Babycham introduced the Babycham Babe beauty contest; when it was revived in 1997 the winner was model, marathon-runner and *I'm a Celebrity … Get Me Out of Here!* contestant Nell McAndrew.

Bell's Blended Scotch Whisky – a quality dram since 1904

A spirit distilled from malted grain, whisky is a truly international beverage with devoted fans as far apart as Argentina and Japan. Curiously, though, in order to tell the story of the UK's leading whisky brand it is necessary to begin with a name more commonly associated with port. In 1825 one Thomas Sandeman began trading in whisky and tea from premises in the Kirkgate, Perth. Twelve years later he was doing well enough to need the services of a young salesman, a talented young man called Arthur Bell. By 1851 Bell had achieved partner status in the enterprise and was conducting experiments in combining several different whiskies to create a special blend.

When Bell's two sons, Arthur Kinmond and Robert, joined the business in 1895 the firm became known as Bell's & Sons but their whisky products carried names such as Scotch Fir and Colleen Old Scotch Whisky. Although his sons were keen to establish their name as a brand, Bell Senior resisted the idea. He died in 1900 but perhaps out of respect for his wishes, it was to be another four years before the Bell's name appeared on one of their bottles of whisky.

In 1925 the phrase 'Afore ye go' made its debut on bottles of Bell's; according to some sources, it referenced the bottles of whisky given to young men employed in the whisky trade as they headed off to the trenches in the First World War. During the Twenties the whisky producers were severely hit by the far-reaching effects of American Prohibition but the firm of Arthur Bell & Sons managed to ride out the storm. In 1933, when Prohibition was repealed, it made sure it was ready to take advantage of the inevitable business boom by acquiring three new distilleries including the famous Blair Athol. Difficult times returned during the Second World War but again Bell's managed to stay afloat, even though Arthur Kinmond and Robert Bell both died in 1942. After the war the new chairman, W. G. Farquharson, set the wheels in motion for an ambitious expansion programme which continued throughout the Seventies and Eighties. Today visitors can learn more about malt whisky production by taking a tour at the Blair Athol Visitor Centre.

At the time of writing Bell's is owned by Diageo plc, a multinational alcoholic beverage company formed in 1997 by the merger of Guinness and Grand Metropolitan.

Did you know … ?

Whisky is spelled differently depending on where it is produced. Purely by coincidence, it seems a general rule of thumb that for countries with an E in their names - Ireland and the United States of America, for example - the spelling is <u>whiskey</u> whereas for those without one, such as Scotland and Canada, it is <u>whisky</u>.

Coca-Cola – the real thing since 1886

Like it or not, there can be no denying that Coca-Cola is the world's most iconic soft drink brand. Indeed, some might go further than that and argue that it is the world's most iconic product. Yet in its first year of production, just nine glasses of the beverage were sold every day. Contrast that figure with today's 1.9 billion daily servings of Coca-Cola products and it's fair to say that the caramel-coloured drink has come a very long way from its humble origins in nineteenth-century Atlanta.

Back in 1886, an Atlanta-based pharmacist called John Stith Pemberton was experimenting with different ingredients including sugar and a variety of spices when he created a liquid that he thought had potential. Taking his syrupy mixture to the nearby Jacob's Pharmacy, he watched as it was combined with carbonated water to form a unique drink. When the customers who first sampled it indicated their approval, Pemberton's creation went on sale at the Jacob's Pharmacy soda fountain, priced at five cents a glass, with a name provided by Pemberton's bookkeeper, Frank Robinson. Robinson also wrote out the name in Spencerian script, an elaborate calligraphy style much-used in America at that time. A legendary brand had just been born.

Interest grew as word spread about the new drink, and by 1891 an Atlanta businessman called Asa Candler had acquired the rights to the Coca-Cola brand. A gifted salesman, Candler used innovative techniques such as complimentary coupons and assertive branding to promote his product. It worked, because by 1895 there were factories producing Coca-Cola syrup in Chicago, Dallas and Los Angeles. Before long Coca-Cola had expanded into overseas markets including Canada, Cuba, Puerto Rico and the UK where it arrived in 1900, brought by Asa Candler's son Charles on a visit to England. When competitors began to produce copycat brands, Coca-Cola responded by

Did you know ... ?

During the Second World War, American servicemen all over the world were able to buy a bottle of Coca-Cola for just five cents thanks to a directive from the company's president, Robert Woodruff.

urging their customers to 'Demand the genuine' and 'Accept no substitute'. To further distinguish itself from the copycat brands, from 1916 Coca-Cola was issued in the iconic 'Contour Bottle' shape which was designed by the Root Glass Company from Indiana.

Although the drink had already spread to a number of countries by the start of the Second World War, many people enjoyed their first taste of Coca-Cola during the conflict via the US soldiers serving in their countries. Building on this, once the war was over the company increased its global operations. At the same time, at home in the USA the bubbly drink was chiming perfectly with the post-war mood of carefree optimism. Both nationally and internationally, Coca-Cola had arrived and made it abundantly clear that it was here to stay.

While the original Coca-Cola remains the flagship product, new brands have been introduced since the 1950s. Of these, the best known in the UK market has to be Diet Coke which was launched in the USA in 1982 and arrived in Britain the following year.

Gordon's – refreshingly dry since 1769

In 1769, Alexander Gordon's nearest and dearest probably questioned his wisdom when he chose to open a gin distillery in Southwark on London's south bank. At the time, gin had a decidedly dodgy reputation; all too often the juniper berry-based spirit was adulterated with turpentine and other unhealthy substances. Nevertheless, it was irresistible to the poor and destitute because it offered a cheap route to temporary oblivion.

Although the Gin Act of 1751 had sought to regulate the industry, gin quality remained unreliable when Alexander Gordon entered the game. Little seems to be known about him apart from the fact that he was of Scottish descent and had a mission to produce a truly excellent gin. Eschewing inferior ingredients, he combined juniper berries with grain liquor and a secret mixture of botanicals to create a flavourful gin of the highest quality. In 1786 he relocated his enterprise to Clerkenwell, an area of London renowned for its abundant water supply.

By 1800, having found favour with the navy, Gordon's London Dry Gin was being carried around the world where it soon attracted new admirers. In 1823 Alexander

Did you know ... ?

During the eighteenth century gin was often referred to as geneva or jeneva; the name derived from *'genièvre'*, the French word for juniper, which in turn was altered to *'genever'* by the Dutch from whom the English acquired a taste for the spirit when it was brought over by William of Orange.

Gordon's son Charles took over the business, having first served a seven-year apprenticeship in order to learn the ropes. He remained at the helm until 1898 when the company merged with Charles Tanqueray & Co to become Tanqueray Gordon & Co. When Charles Gordon died the following year, the firm's ties with the Gordon family were cut. In 1904 a distinctive new bottle was introduced for Gordon's gin; green and square-faced, for the first time it had the word 'Dry' on its label, referencing the fact that the spirit was unsweetened.

Owned today by Diageo, Gordon's is now produced in Scotland. The world's best-selling premium gin, it holds a Royal Warrant from the Queen.

Guinness – Dublin's pride since 1759

In 1759, a decade before Alexander Gordon opened his gin distillery in Southwark, Arthur Guinness, a small-scale ale brewer from County Kildare, founded a brewery at St. James's Gate in Dublin. In a gesture of magnificent optimism, Guinness signed a 9,000-year lease for the site at an annual rent of £45. The first output from the new brewery was something called Guinness Dublin Ale but by the 1770s he had decided to try his hand at creating his own version of porter. This was a dark beer which Guinness had first encountered on a visit to London and was named for the London market porters for whom it was a favourite thirst-quencher. When his new brew overtook Dublin Ale in popularity, Guinness ceased ale production and threw all his resources into the Guinness Porter.

Arthur Guinness died in 1803 but his brewery continued, with the fame of its porter spreading far and wide. Gradually, as its colour became deep black rather than dark brown and its recipe evolved to one of roasted barley, hops and yeast, Guinness began to be known as stout rather than porter – stout being another dark beer but with a lower malt, higher roasted barley content than straightforward porter.

Did you know...?

The original copy for the famous Guinness toucan advertisements was written by crime writer Dorothy L. Sayers when she worked as a copywriter for Guinness's London advertising agency, S. H. Benson.

Following years of experimentation, Draught Guinness became available in the 1960s, followed in 1987 by the introduction of canned Guinness. This was only made possible when the company invented the widget, a plastic device which works with CO_2 to enable the creamy Guinness head to develop as the drink is poured from the can. Owned today by Diageo, Guinness is brewed in more than fifty countries worldwide (including Ireland, of course) and is sold in 150 or so. Fans can discover more about Guinness (and enjoy a drop of the black stuff) by booking a tour of the Guinness Storehouse, the visitor centre at the St. James's Gate Brewery.

Harvey's Bristol Cream – making Christmas merry since 1882

For many, Christmas just isn't Christmas without a bottle of sherry – a fortified wine made from the white grapes of Jerez de la Frontera in Spain – to keep out the winter chills. And for the majority of people, the sherry of choice will be Harvey's Bristol Cream, the leading sherry brand both in the UK and globally.

The brand sprang into existence in 1882 but its roots go back as far as 1796 when a wine merchant called William Perry set up shop on the site of a thirteenth-century Augustinian monastery. It was an ideal location because when ships laden with wine arrived from Spain, Perry's employees were able to manoeuvre the casks down a series of underground tunnels that linked the nearby docks to the monastery's old cellars.

In 1822 John Harvey, the nephew of Perry's partner, joined the venture as an apprentice, taking his uncle's place in the business in due course. During the Peninsula War of 1807 to 1814, the sherry trade had been severely disrupted by warfare but once Napoleon was vanquished the situation began to improve. By the 1840s, Perry's cellars were full of Spanish and Portuguese wines and Harvey was a married man with eight children, three of whom followed him into the business. Two of them, John and Edward, developed a new blend of sherry in the 1860s. The story goes that one day a grand lady was sampling a popular rich dark sherry known as Bristol Milk. She was then invited by the Harvey brothers to taste their new dessert blend and, having done so, pronounced, 'If that be milk, then this is cream'. Thus was a brand name born, although Bristol Cream was not registered as a trademark until 1882.

When John Harvey acquired senior partner status in 1871 he changed the company name to John Harvey & Sons. Having remained a private, family-run firm for four generations, it went public in 1958 and was acquired by Showerings (of Babycham fame) in 1966. At the time of writing the brand was owned by Beam Suntory but a change of ownership was anticipated in the early part of 2016.

IRN-BRU – Scotland's second drink since 1901

Fizzy and gingery-orange in colour, Scotland's favourite non-alcoholic beverage is that rarest of entities, a brand still in the hands of the family firm responsible for its creation. Launched in 1901 by A G Barr, a second generation soft drinks manufacturer, IRN-BRU was known initially as Strachan Brew before changing to Iron Brew. A further change of name was necessitated in 1946 when the USA passed the Lanham Act prohibiting false descriptions in trademarks; since the drink was not actually brewed, the name Iron Brew would infringe the new law. As a result, when the law came into effect in 1947, the drink had been renamed IRN-BRU.

While it is known that IRN-BRU contains thirty-two different flavours, the precise recipe is a closely-guarded secret which is passed down through the Barr family. At the present, three people are privy to the secret; two of them are members of the Barr family while the identity of the third is confidential.

Today, sales of IRN-BRU in Scotland are more or less equal to those of Coca-Cola. More surprisingly, perhaps, is the fact that the brand is the third bestselling non-alcoholic beverage across the UK. It also has a strong following in parts of Europe, Africa and Asia, and is produced under licence in Canada, the USA and Norway as well as in Russia where it is manufactured by the Moscow Brewing Company. In Scotland, meanwhile, the IRN-BRU plant in Cumbernauld has the capacity to produce 690 million cans annually.

Did you know … ?

Until as recently as 2015, IRN-BRU customers were able to reclaim a deposit of 30p for the return of their 750ml glass bottles; the practice, established in 1905 when the deposit was one halfpenny, was discontinued in December 2015 due to a significant drop in uptake caused by customers choosing to recycle their bottles instead.

Lucozade – orange energy since 1927

Once upon a time, childhood bouts of illness were brightened by the prospect of a Lucozade-fuelled convalescence. Thanks to the famous advertising slogan, everyone knew that the drink – sweet, fizzy and luminously orange – could be relied upon to aid recovery. Trusted by mothers and recommended by doctors when solid food was inadvisable, Lucozade was the sickroom drink par excellence.

This carbonated elixir was the creation of William Owen, a chemist from Barras Bridge, Newcastle. Already the owner of a mineral water factory, in 1927 Owen developed the glucose syrup drink as a means of providing the weak and ailing with an energy boost. Its first name was Glucozade but by 1929, when it was to be found in hospitals across Britain, the G had been abandoned.

In 1938 Lucozade was acquired by Beechams, of Beechams Powders fame. In 1989 the Beecham Group merged with SmithKline Beckman to become SmithKline Beecham which in turn merged with Glaxo Wellcome in 2000 to form GlaxoSmithKline. In 2013 Lucozade ownership changed again when GlaxoSmithKline off-loaded a few of its soft drinks brands to Suntory, the Japanese brewing and distilling outfit. However, it is still made in the UK, in Coleford in the Forest of Dean, to be precise.

Long before this, however, Lucozade underwent a significant brand repositioning. In 1983 the famous 'Lucozade aids recovery' slogan was abandoned although its counterpart, the long-running 'Lucozade replaces lost energy', remained. At the same time plastic bottles were introduced as replacements for the familiar glass bottles with their colourful, shiny wrappings, and new flavours were created. The energy message was reinforced when Olympic decathlete Daley Thompson was signed to promote the brand, followed in 1990 by the launch of Lucozade Sport with endorsements from leading sporting figures such as John Barnes, Alan Shearer and Jonny Wilkinson. Actually, this wasn't an entirely new strategy for Lucozade since back in 1954 motor racing legend Stirling Moss endorsed the original version in a series of print advertisements.

Relatively unknown outside its home market, in the UK Lucozade remains the leading brand in the energy drinks category.

Pimm's No. 1 Cup – quintessentially English since 1823

As integral to a traditional English summer as strawberries and cream and Wimbledon and rain, the alcoholic fruit cup known as Pimm's No. 1 was created in 1823 by James Pimm, the owner of a London oyster bar. Pimm's concoction, originally intended as a digestive tonic and made from a gin base with the addition of herbs, fruits and other ingredients, was served in small, 'No. 1' tankards. Situated near the Bank of England, Pimm's bar was patronised by affluent business types who sampled the intriguing new drink with gusto. Word spread, demand increased and by 1851 Pimm was bottling the drink and selling it for consumption in other establishments.

In 1865 Pimm sold up but his drinks business continued to thrive. Over time new varieties based on other spirits were introduced: the whisky-based Pimm's No. 2 and rum-based No. 4 failed to achieve longevity but the brandy-based No. 3 has now been rebranded as Pimm's Winter Cup and the vodka-based No. 6 has recently been brought out of retirement.

Did you know...?

In 2003 Pimm's launched its famous 'Pimm's O'Clock' campaign with actor and *Pointless* presenter Alexander Armstrong playing an upper class twit in the TV ads.

Ribena – bursting with blackcurrants since 1938

This popular blackcurrant-flavoured children's favourite was developed in 1938 by two men. The first was Frank Armstrong of H. W. Carter & Co., a Bristol-based firm which produced mineral waters and lemon cordials and was owned by Armstrong's family, and the second was Dr Vernon Charley from Bristol University's former Long Ashton Research Station. Originally conceived as a cordial to be added to milk surpluses to create milkshakes, the blackcurrant-based product was found by Charley to be naturally rich in Vitamin C. Playing up to its healthy properties, Armstrong gave it a name inspired by *ribes negrum*, the scientific term name for blackcurrants.

It was largely good timing that gave Ribena success as a commercial brand. When oranges and other citrus fruits became impossible to buy during the Second World War, the Government needed to find a home-grown source of Vitamin C. Blackcurrant-rich Ribena was the obvious solution so in 1942 virtually the entire British blackcurrant crop was sent to H. W. Carter & Co for conversion into the cordial. It was then given to the nation's children and mums-to-be. In 1947 production moved to Coleford in Gloucestershire where Ribena is still made to this day. Together with Lucozade, the brand was acquired by Suntory in 2013.

Did you know ... ?

In 1982 Ribena became the first branded squash to be made available as a ready-to-drink product.

Robinsons Barley Water – serving up squash since 1935

According to a study conducted in 2013, in the UK we consume around 15 million glasses of Robinsons every day. The figure demonstrates that even in the age of vegetable smoothies and zero-calorie pops, many of us remain in the grips of a love affair with good old-fashioned fruit squash.

The roots of that love affair stretch back to 1823 when Matthias Archibald Robinson, the son of a London grocer, began manufacturing Patent Barley and Groats (the hulled kernels of various grains) in powdered form. When mixed with hot water, the powder formed a drink believed to be beneficial to invalids and nursing mothers. Robinson died in 1837 but the company he founded continued to thrive. In 1862 it merged with mustard producers Keen and Sons and then in 1903 was acquired by Colmans, the biggest name in the mustard market.

This was the state of play in 1934 when a sales representative called Eric Smedley Hodgson mixed Patent Barley Crystals with lemon juice, sugar and water to create a refreshing and hydrating drink for the players at Wimbledon that year. The drink

---

Did you know … ?

Robinsons Barley Water has been Wimbledon's official soft drink since 1935.

---

proved so popular that in excess of 250 gallons were served during that one tournament. Robinsons Lemon Barley Water had arrived. Since then, many different flavours have been added to the product portfolio including Orange, Apple & Blackcurrant and Summer Fruits. Since 1995 the Robinsons brand has been owned by Britvic, the British soft drinks company based in Hemel Hempstead.

Schweppes – bubbly and soft since 1783

Pop, soda or fizzy drink: call it what you will, it's a carbonated beverage and as such it owes a huge debt to a Swiss watchmaker called Johann Jacob Schweppe. A keen amateur scientist, when Schweppe wasn't creating precision timepieces he liked nothing better than to tinker about in a laboratory; in 1783 he was doing just that when came up with an efficient process for carbonating water. He went into commercial production in Geneva that same year but in 1792 moved the operation to London's Drury Lane. In 1834 the company was bought by John Kemp-Welch, a wine merchant from Bath, and his friend, the unfortunately-named William Evill. Under their ownership a brand-new product, a fizzy lemonade, was launched. It proved so successful that the floodgates were opened for a slew of differently flavoured carbonated drinks. Yet the firm's biggest breakthrough came in 1870 when it introduced Indian Tonic Water, a carbonated drink with quinine added for its health benefits. People soon discovered that the rather bitter taste of the Tonic Water was radically improved by the addition of gin and thus the legendary gin and tonic was born.

It wasn't until 1957 that a Schweppes product came along to rival the success of its Tonic Water; during its heady first couple of years, Bitter Lemon actually outperformed the brand's flagship product before the nation's G&T drinkers ensured that the natural order was restored. In the Sixties Schweppes achieved household name status with the 'Schhh ... You Know Who' commercials starring the late William Franklin.

In 1969 Schweppes became Cadbury Schweppes when it merged with the confectionery heavyweight. This led to some major acquisitions including Dr Pepper, 7-Up and Snapple, and when Schweppes split from Cadbury in 2008 it was renamed the Dr Pepper Snapple Group.

Smirnoff Vodka – premium purity since 1864

Taking its name from the Russian word for water, vodka is a spirit traditionally made from distilled rye, wheat or even potatoes. In Russia it has been helping to keep out the cold for hundreds of years although in the early days it would have been distilled at home by peasants for their personal consumption. When commercial distilleries began producing it, the impure quality of the spirit needed the addition of herb and fruit flavourings to make it more palatable. The situation didn't alter much until the nineteenth century when Pyotr Smirnov devised a recipe for the purest possible vodka.

Smirnov's story is one of remarkable contrasts. Born into serfdom in an agricultural community around 200 miles from Russia, when he died in 1898 he was said to be one of the richest men in the country. It was the freeing of the serfs by Tsar Alexander II in 1861 that enabled Smirnov to begin his ascent but he achieved his extraordinary success through his own talent and drive. In 1864 when he started to distil vodka he dreamed of creating a product of such purity that it would be endorsed by the Tsar

himself. Having come up with a special recipe and purification system, he promoted his product by paying Moscow's beggars to ask for his particular vodka brand at the drinking establishments they frequented. The strategy worked and within less than a decade his sales were bringing in an annual revenue of 600,000 roubles. His life's ambition was achieved in 1886 when he became the Tsar's official vodka supplier.

Smirnov's son Vladimir ran the company following his father's death. When the Bolsheviks came to power he fled to France where he proved himself a chip off the old block by re-establishing the business. Now called Smirnoff, the French version of Smirnov, the vodka became a bestseller across Europe and the USA. Owned today by Diageo and made in a number of countries including the UK, Smirnoff is the world's bestselling premium distilled spirit.

Gone but not forgotten: Corona

Corona was a fizzy drinks brand that originated in Wales in the 1920s and was sold door-to-door across the UK for decades. Although it ceased to exist in 1987, a memorial exists in the form of the old Porth factory which has been converted into a recording studio called The Pop Factory.

Honourable mention: Baileys

First produced in 1974, Baileys Original Irish Cream has already become a firm favourite with consumers. Its success is partly due to clever, consistent advertising but also to the fact that it is undeniably rather delicious. And its Irish credentials are impeccable since every bottle is produced and bottled in the Emerald Isle.

Chapter 3

The Tuck Box

Generations of British children have chomped their way through untold quantities of these legendary confectionery brands, to the delight of their taste buds and the detriment of their dental health. In the old-fashioned sweet shops, where floor-to-ceiling shelves were lined with jars containing boiled sweets in garish colours, customers tended to ask for their choices by type rather than brand: a quarter of pear drops, half a pound of toffee bonbons and so on. Elsewhere, however – in newsagents, corner shops and, in time, in the new-fangled supermarkets – the mass-produced chocolate bars and packets of sugary sweets were in demand thanks in large part to the clever advertising that made them household names. Our grandparents grew up with these sweets and now our own offspring and their children are enjoying them, too. Yes, these are the confectionery diehards, so hardwired into our DNA that we couldn't imagine life without them.

Aero – chocolate bubbles since 1935

Created by Rowntree, one of York's great confectionery firms which was founded by Joseph Rowntree in the nineteenth century, Aero was launched in the north of England in 1935. Costing two old pennies, it was hailed as the 'new chocolate' on account of its unique bubbly texture. Such was its success that by 1936 Aero was selling across the UK and had even made it to New York.

Aero has been available in various flavours over the years – who knew there had once been a Nut Milk variety? – but the consistent bestsellers are Peppermint and Milk Chocolate. When Rowntree began advertising Aero on television in the 1950s, its place in the British confectionery hall of fame was cemented. Today Aero is owned by Nestlé.

Did you know … ?

With air travel becoming increasingly popular in the 1930s, Rowntree originally intended to call their new bubbly chocolate product Airways.

Bassett's Liquorice Allsorts – mismatched favourites since 1899

Launched in 1899 by George Bassett & Co, a Sheffield confectionery manufacturer established half a century earlier, Liquorice Allsorts are colourful sweets made from sugar, liquorice and coconut mixed with assorted flavourings and formed into bite-sized cubes and discs. According to company legend, their mismatched appearance came about by chance when a sales representative managed to muddle a tray of samples whilst presenting them to a customer. Delighted by their novel appearance, the customer placed an order and Liquorice Allsorts were born.

The sweet's status as a minor national treasure was cemented in 1929 when Greenlys, one of the leading advertising agencies of the time, created Bertie Bassett, a mascot character composed of a number different Liquorice Allsorts. He is still promoting the brand today which, after changing ownership a number of times, currently belongs to Mondelēz.

Bounty – tropical tropes since 1951

The Bounty bar, that lushly sweet marriage of coconut and chocolate that tends to divide opinion almost as much as Marmite, was launched in the UK in 1951. Created by the Mars confectionery company, initially it was available only in milk chocolate although a dark chocolate variety was introduced a short while later. It is easy to differentiate between the two varieties because the milk chocolate comes in a blue wrapper and the dark chocolate in red.

A distinctive feature of the Bounty is that it comes in two separate sections which used to nestle snugly within a little cardboard tray. While the cardboard has been consigned to history, the claim that Bounty offers a taste of paradise lives on.

Cadbury's Dairy Milk – milky magic since 1905

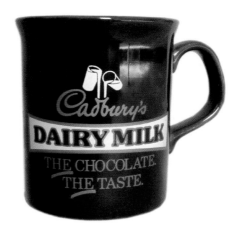

The Cadbury manufacturing story began in 1831 when a Birmingham shopkeeper called John Cadbury started to produce cocoa and drinking chocolate. In 1861 John's sons, George and Richard, took over the business, using an inheritance from their mother to finance the enterprise during a problematic period. Their commitment was rewarded when, in 1866, an expensive new piece of machinery enabled them to create the UK's first unadulterated cocoa powder, Cadbury's Cocoa Essence.

In 1875 Cadbury created their first Easter eggs but it wasn't until 1897 that they ventured into the production of milk chocolate. Rather coarse and dry, their initial product was inferior to the Swiss chocolate that was dominating the market. Keen to improve, in 1905 Cadbury launched Dairy Milk, a milk chocolate bar with a uniquely high content of milk. The first packaging was pale mauve with red script but in 1920 it was replaced by the purple we are familiar with today. The public showed their appreciation for the new chocolate brand by making it the UK's bestseller by the start of the 1920s.

Introduced in 1928, the famous 'glass and a half full of milk' symbol is still in use today. As of 2015, the brand is owned by Mondelēz.

Crunchie – that Friday feeling since 1929

Bars of golden honeycomb covered in creamy milk chocolate, Crunchies are bigger today than they used to be, having been given a size increase in 1982. Created in 1929 by Fry's, the Bristol-based confectioners who amalgamated with their rival Cadbury ten years earlier, Crunchie was the British answer to a similar Australian product called Violet Crumble.

In recent years, the slogans 'Thank Crunchie it's Friday' and 'Get that Friday feeling' have been associated with the product.

Did you know ... ?

Crunchies make an appearance in *National Velvet*, Enid Bagnold's much-loved novel which was published in 1935. In the text the treat is described as a 'chocolate stick' and beneath the chocolate there is a 'sort of honeycomb, crisp and friable, something between biscuit and burnt sugar'.'

Flake – crumbliest chocolate since 1920

Legend has it that Cadbury owe the development of their popular Flake bar to a vigilant employee. This unnamed individual observed that when liquid chocolate was poured into moulds to create other products, the excess always overran the sides, trickling downwards in a molten flow. The result, when the flow had cooled and set, was a multi-layered chocolate stick with a tendency to crumble and flake. It went on sale in 1920 and a major milestone was reached ten years later with the advent of the Flake 99, a harmonious marriage of soft white ice cream and the crumbly chocolate bar.

Initially, Flake was marketed in a transparent wrapper and described as 'flaky Cadbury Dairy Milk that just crumbles on your tongue'. In 1959, when the yellow wrapper that is still in use today first appeared, the brand was considered strong enough to stand on its own without the Dairy Milk appellation. However, it was in the Seventies that Flake made a lasting impact on the public consciousness with the memorable TV commercials featuring attractive young women eating the chocolate bar, accompanied by a song with the following lyrics: 'Only the crumbliest, flakiest chocolate, tastes like chocolate never tasted before'.

Did you know ... ?

More than 100 million Flake 99s are sold every year.

Fry's Turkish Delight – Eastern promise since 1914

Turkish delight – little cubes of sweet jelly subtly infused with the flavours of the Middle East – is another of those confections that divide opinion; many love it, many more cannot abide it (Edmund in *The Lion, the Witch and the Wardrobe* loved it, but that didn't turn out so well for him). Therefore, it might seem a tad surprising that Fry's Turkish Delight has survived in a highly competitive marketplace for over a century.

Introduced in 1914, five years before J. S. Fry's acquisition by Cadbury, the product consists of small slabs of rose-flavoured Turkish delight encased in milk chocolate. Its longevity possibly owes something to a memorable advertising slogan. Since the Fifties, the phrase 'full of Eastern Promise' has been used to imbue the product with exotic allure despite the fact that it used to be made near Bristol and is now produced in Poland.

Kit Kat – chocolate break of choice since 1935

Kit Kat first appeared on the market in 1935; within two years it had become Rowntree's bestselling product, a position it retains to this day. Back then it was known as Rowntree's Chocolate Crisp, changing to Kit Kat Chocolate Crisp in 1937 before settling down simply as Kit Kat after the Second World War. Created at Rowntree's Haxby Road confectionery factory in York, the chocolate-coated wafer fingers were tried out in London and the South East before being rolled out across the nation. From the very beginning they were available in two-finger and four-finger variations.

Over the years advertising campaigns have come and gone but the one that has left the deepest impression on the public is the slogan 'Have a break … have a Kit Kat' which was first used in 1958. Although Rowntree was acquired by global confectionery giants Nestlé in 1988, Kit Kat is still made today in York.

Did you know … ?

In 1945 Kit Kat swapped its red and white livery for a blue wrapper when it had to be made with plain rather than milk chocolate due to milk shortages. When the milk chocolate variety returned in 1947, the red and white wrapper returned but consumers had to wait until 1997 for the return of a dark chocolate Kit Kat.

Maltesers – reduced-guilt confectionery since 1936

The 'chocolate with the less fattening centre' was created in 1936 by Forrest Mars, son of Mars, Inc founder Frank Mars. Forrest came to the UK in 1932, set up a confectionery operation in Slough and a few years later came up with the  irresistible combination of malted milk balls coated in milk chocolate.

For years, the brand's lightness and its comparatively low calorie count (less than 190 per packet) have been the focus of press and TV campaigns. In recent years, a number of well-known comedy actresses including Katherine Parkinson (*Humans*, *The IT Crowd*, *Doc Martin*), Amanda Abbington (*Mr Selfridge*, *Sherlock*) and Ingrid Oliver (*Doctor Who*, *Material Girl*, *Watson & Oliver*) have starred in a series of quirkily humorous ads.

Did you know ... ?

US confectioners Hershey's market a malted milk ball product called Malteser. Bearing a close resemblance to Mars' Maltesers and sold in a similar red packet, it was the subject of a recent legal wrangle which was settled amicably out of court in 2015.

Mars – helping us work, rest and play since 1932

Every day, three million Mars bars are produced at the Mars factory in Slough, a fact that encourages many to regard it as the undisputed king of all chocolate bars. A lushly layered creation of sticky caramel and soft nougat surrounded by milk chocolate, it was the first product created by Forrest Mars when he came to England in 1932 and opened a small confectionery outfit in Slough. Legend has it that with limited funds at his disposal, Forrest and his team of between four and twelve employees (accounts differ as to the actual number) perfected his recipe in a small kitchen stocked with second-hand equipment. Although not identical, the formula was closely based on his father Frank Mars' Milky Way which was already an established brand in America. This should not be confused with the UK version of the Milky Way (see below). When the Mars bar went into production in August 1932 it was coated in chocolate obtained from Cadbury since the fledgling Slough site was some way off being ready to produce its own chocolate.

During the Second World War Mars bars were given to British troops and sent to prisoners of war in Germany. In 1959, the famous 'A Mars a day helps you work, rest and play' slogan was used for the first time. A variation of the same phrase is still used today. In recent years Mars has become an official supporter of the England football team and an official sponsor of the Scotland team.

> **Did you know … ?**
>
> In 1955 Petula Clark and the late Bob Monkhouse appeared in the first Mars bar TV commercial.

Milkybar – the creamiest milk, the whitest bar, since 1936

Launched in 1936, Milkybar is Nestlé Confectionery's eleventh oldest brand. It is also the UK's best-selling white chocolate bar and in 2007 became the first confectionery brand to be made exclusively from natural ingredients.

However, the thing most people remember about the product is the Milkybar Kid, the pistol-toting, horse-riding, white chocolate munching cowboy child who has promoted the brand on and off since 1961. In that time, the Milkybar Kid has been portrayed in television commercials by ten different child actors, all of them blond, cute, bespectacled and possibly destined to be haunted by the Milky Bar song for years to come. All together now: 'The Milkybars are on me!'

Milky Way – not spoiling appetites since 1932

Created in America in 1923 by Frank Mars, the first confectionery bar to go by the name of Milky Way has a chocolate-nougat base which is covered with a layer of caramel and then coated all over with milk chocolate. If that sounds a lot like the bar we know in the UK as a Mars, it's because Frank Mars allowed his son Forrest to make use of his Milky Way formula when he came to the UK in 1932 to set up a European confectionery empire (see Mars bar, above).

Straightforward enough so far? Well hold on, because things are about to become slightly more confusing. That's because the milk chocolate-coated whipped nougat bar known in the UK as a Milky Way is actually a very close cousin of the 3 Musketeers bar, another Mars product which was launched in the US in 1932. Three years later the similar Milky Way went on sale in Britain.

Perhaps the most famous advertising slogan associated with the Milky Way is 'the sweet you can eat between meals without ruining your appetite'.

Quality Street – sweetening Christmas since 1936

Quality Street is the world's number one selling boxed chocolate assortment. It is reckoned that around 6,000 individual sweets are produced every minute; put another way, that's 67 million per week. Although huge, the number isn't altogether surprising given the stampede to stock up on these devilishly tempting sweeties that takes place in supermarkets across the nation the moment the first hint of Christmas scents the air; around October, in other words. Yet without the efforts of a hardworking couple from Halifax in the 1890s, our Yuletides would be bereft of green noisette triangles, golden toffee pennies, 'the purple one' (allegedly the most popular flavour in the Quality Street assortment), and all the other favourites.

Back in 1890, shopkeepers John and Violet Mackintosh hit upon a way to combine traditional English toffee – delicious but potentially jaw-breaking – with soft, gloopy American caramel. After a few years their recipe had become so popular that they closed their shop and opened a toffee factory instead.

By the 1930s, John Mackintosh & Sons Ltd was a thriving confectionery business with over 1,000 employees in Halifax, and a second factory in Norwich which had formerly been known as A. J. Caley & Son. Yet the difficult economic conditions of the era meant that ordinary people had less disposable income for luxuries like boxes of chocolates. Realising this, in 1936 Mackintosh decided to create a range of toffees and sweets which would be coated in chocolate, making them more affordable than confectionery with a higher chocolate content. By putting the sweets in gaily-coloured wrappers and packaging them in bright, attractive tins, they made their new product look irresistible and by naming it Quality Street they emphasised its excellence. In fact the name was borrowed from a popular J. M. Barrie play and the people dressed in period costume on the original packaging were based on Barrie's characters.

In 1969 Mackintosh merged with York's famous Rowntree firm to become Rowntree Mackintosh; this in turn was acquired by Nestlé nineteen years later. Nevertheless, Quality Street confectionery is still made in Halifax today.

Did you know ... ?

Quality Street's coloured wrappers are biodegradable and can be composted with your garden waste. The foil, meanwhile, can be recycled with your tins.

Rolos – testing love since 1937

A tube of individual milk chocolates filled with caramel, Rolos have been a firm favourite in the UK since their introduction in 1937. Originally a Mackintosh creation, Rolos are now owned by Nestlé and produced in Newcastle upon Tyne. In the US they are made under licence by The Hershey Company thanks to a longstanding arrangement.

'Do you love anyone enough to give them your last Rolo?' – arguably the most memorable Rolo advertising slogan – was first used in 1980.

Rowntree's Fruit Pastilles – fruity chewing since 1881

The oldest sweet in the Rowntree family, Rowntree's Fruit Pastilles were developed in 1881 by a Frenchman called Claude Gaget. A specialist in pastilles – sweet lozenges, often with semi-medicinal qualities, in which the French led the way – Gaget had been brought in by Rowntree two years earlier in order to devise a  quality product that could be sold by pharmacies. His first fruit pastilles, purchased loose from chemists at a penny an ounce, met with such immediate success that the fortunes of the hitherto ailing confectionery firm were turned around. Gaget was also responsible for Rowntree's Fruit Gums which were introduced in 1893 but their best-known catchphrase, 'Don't forget the fruit gums, mum!' dates from 1958.

Manufactured at Fawdon in Tyneside since the 1950s, Rowntree's Fruit Pastilles are sugar-coated and come in five fruit flavours – lemon, lime, blackcurrant, orange and strawberry. Made with real fruit juice, they contain no artificial colours, flavours or preservatives. It is estimated that there are approximately 74 calories in seven of the sweets.

When they were first advertised on television in 1959, their somewhat downbeat catchphrase was 'Yes, now you too can enjoy the best sweets in the world ... Rowntree's Fruit Pastilles!' Things hadn't much improved a couple of years later when their TV ad concluded with the phrase, 'Rowntree's Fruit Pastilles with the tingle tongue taste

— just a thought!' However, with the introduction of the memorable 'All you can do is chew' campaign in the 1980s, Rowntree's Fruit Pastilles finally entered the advertising hall of fame. The brand has been owned by Nestlé since 1988.

> **Did you know...?**
>
> The word *pastille* is French and should be pronounced to rhyme with Bastille. Instead, in the UK pronunciation is usually closer to pastel, as in the colour shade.

Smarties – clever beans since 1882

Generations of British children have experienced the thrill of flipping the top off a cardboard tube of Smarties and pouring out a colourful stream of chocolate beans into their eager little mitts. It's debatable whether their thrill would have been lessened or enhanced by the knowledge that their sweetie of choice was inspired by a French product popularly known as '*crottes de lapin*'. That's 'rabbit droppings' to you and me. Perhaps wisely, when Rowntree of York introduced their version in 1882 they used the term Chocolate Beans instead. This was changed to Smarties in 1937, allegedly because some jobsworth felt misled by the use of the word 'bean'. One can only imagine the kerfuffle if Rowntree had chosen to stick with rabbit droppings.

Currently there are eight colours in the Smartie rainbow: red, orange, green, yellow, pink, violet, brown and blue which was introduced in 1988, originally as a limited edition. Despite the different colours, only one – orange – has a different taste as it is flavoured with natural orange oil. Since 2006 they have contained no artificial colours or flavourings.

Smarties became a Nestlé brand in 1988. They continued to be made at their birthplace in York until 2007 when all production was moved to Germany.

Terry's Chocolate Orange – Christmas stocking fillers since 1931

Like rivals Rowntree, renowned confectionery company Terry's of York had a presence in York that stretched back to the nineteenth century. That was when Joseph Terry the elder began producing all manner of comfits, sweets, lozenges and other edible treats. When his son, another Joseph Terry, inherited the business in 1850 he took it to the next level, moving into larger premises and expanding operations so that by 1867 the company was offering 400 different lines.

In 1923 a new generation of Terrys – Frank and Noel – joined the family business. Under their management the company moved to a purpose-built factory, The Chocolate Works, off Bishopthorpe Road. It was here that the Chocolate Orange was born in

1931, a spin-off from the Chocolate Apple which had been introduced in 1926 and was quietly dropped when its sales were outstripped by the new orange-flavoured product.

As the name implies, Terry's Chocolate Orange is an orange-shaped ball of chocolate which comes wrapped in foil inside a cardboard container. Flavoured with orange oil, it divides into twenty segments which are perfect for sharing at Christmas, the product's peak selling season. Originally produced only in milk chocolate, a number of different varieties have come and gone over the years, the most successful of which appears to have been the dark chocolate version.

Terry's Chocolate Orange has benefited from some enjoyable TV ads, perhaps most memorably with comic actress Dawn French declaring, 'It's not Terry's, it's mine!' Today owned by Mondelēz, since 2005 it has been manufactured in Poland.

Gone but not forgotten: Spangles

Introduced by Mars in 1948 with the innocent slogan 'The sweet way to go gay', Spangles were square-shaped boiled sweets with a circular dip in the centre. They came in a variety of fruity flavours as well as some more unusual ones including orangeade, butterscotch and liquorice.

And staying with Mars, let's not overlook Marathon which was created by the confectionery giant in the US in 1930. There it was named Snickers after a horse

---

Did you know … ?

In 1970 Terry's launched a Chocolate Lemon in plain chocolate; it did not find favour with the public and soon vanished from the shelves.

---

but in the UK it was sold as Marathon until 1990 when the American name was adopted. A similar fate befell another Mars product; Opal Fruits were introduced to the British market in 1960 but when they went on sale in the US in 1967 their name was changed to Starburst. In 1998 Mars decreed that in the UK, Opal Fruits should henceforward be known by their American name.

Honourable mentions: Twix & Curly Wurly

Both Twix (introduced by Mars in 1967) and Curly Wurly (launched by Cadbury in 1971) are well on their way to achieving confectionery longevity.

Chapter 4

The Fridge and Freezer

In our current era of chilled ready meals and freezers stuffed with ice cream and fish fingers, it seems extraordinary that a whole stratum of the UK food market was only made possible by the arrival of the refrigerator and its younger sibling, the freezer. For the first half of the twentieth century, most British consumers had little choice but to store their perishable goods – milk, cheese, meat, fish etc – in the coolest part of the house, often a larder but sometimes just a shelf positioned as far as possible from heat sources. Meat might be stored in wooden cupboards fitted with mesh to allow air to circulate; these 'meat safes' kept flies away but weren't especially successful at keeping the produce cool and fresh. As a result, most people shopped on a daily basis, buying only what was needed for that day's meals.

After the Second World War, the situation began to change but at a somewhat sluggish rate. In 1948 only 2 per cent of the UK population possessed a fridge; by 1959 that figure had increased to 13 per cent. Compare that with the USA where, at the same date, a staggering 96 per cent of homes boasted a fridge. It wasn't until 1970 that fridges could be found in the majority of British houses and even then the figure was just 58 per cent.

Nevertheless, once the fridge had fully arrived in the UK its domination was total. Today no one would contemplate managing without one and much the same is true for the freezer, which we accepted with significantly greater alacrity than we had the refrigerator. Just 3 per cent of the population owned a freezer in 1969 but within twenty-six years, 96 per cent of households were enjoying their benefits. And with so many shiny new fridges and freezes waiting to be filled, a galaxy of branded perishable products appeared on the market, changing our shopping and eating habits forever.

Anchor Butter – spreading the word since 1886

Anchor, the famous New Zealand butter brand, has closer roots with Britain than people might imagine. For a start, it was created by a Cornishman, Henry Chidley Reynolds, who emigrated to New Zealand with his family in 1868 when he was 19 years old. For the first few years he worked on his family's vast farm but by the 1880s he was running a dairy farm in Waikato. It was at this point that he met a neighbouring farmer, an American called David Gemmell, who produced a butter that Reynolds liked very much. Gemmell was set to return to the USA but Reynolds persuaded him to delay long enough to help him set up his own butter production operation. Legend has it that the butter's brand name was inspired by a tattoo on the arm of one of Reynold's employees.

Initially the butter was sold to the home market but before long it was being exported to Australia and Hong Kong. After winning an award for Anchor at the Centennial International Exhibition in Melbourne in 1888, Reynolds felt the time was right to begin exporting to the UK. In 1896 he sold the operation to the New Zealand Dairy Association and went to live in Argentina where he set up the River Plate Dairy Company. He died in England in 1925.

Today the Anchor Butter brand is owned by Arla Foods. In 2012 Arla moved production of the butter from New Zealand to Westbury in Wiltshire and thus the story has come full circle.

Birds Eye – the big freeze since 1924

Clarence Birdseye was the father of the frozen food industry, at least as far as the consumer end of the market is concerned. Exporters had been freezing food prior to shipment for some time before he began experimenting with freezing techniques but it was his vision that led to frozen foods becoming an integral part of our eating habits.

Born in Brooklyn in 1886, Birdseye trained as a taxidermist but his observational skills led him to the realisation that fish stayed fresh when rapidly frozen in Arctic waters. Acutely conscious of the commercial possibilities of his discovery, in 1924 he established the General Seafoods Corporation, having first patented the Birdseye Plate Froster. Five years later his company and patents were bought by a trading alliance that was shortly to become General Foods. Pocketing the cool (pun intended) $22 million purchase price, Birdseye moved on to other interests; when he died in 1956, he was in possession of hundreds of patents.

In 1930, meanwhile, frozen fish, meat and vegetables went on sale for the first time under the Birds Eye Frozen Foods trade name. During the 1940s Unilever acquired the rights to the Birds Eye brand everywhere except the USA, and in 1945 a factory for freezing peas and herrings was opened in Great Yarmouth. The Fifties brought a new production unit in Lowestoft as well as the introduction of the fish finger, while the Sixties gave us the original incarnation of Captain Birdseye, a jolly, fish finger-loving seafarer with a West Country twang. From 1967 until 1998 he was portrayed in the television adverts by the late John Hewer. When Birds Eye decided to dispense with the salty old seadog in 1971, an obituary describing the fictitious character as a celebrity and gourmet appeared in *The Times*. He was, it went on to say, 'Mourned by Sea-Cook Jim and the Commodore, in recognition of his selfless devotion to the nutritional needs of the nation's children.' Three years later Birds Eye changed their minds and Captain Birdseye was resurrected.

In 2006 Unilever sold Birds Eye and another frozen food brand called Iglo to Permira, a private equity group. As part of Iglo Foods Holdings, Birds Eye was bought by Nomad Holdings, an American investment group, in April 2015.

Did you know ... ?

In 2010 Birds Eye estimated that their products are eaten by 4.2 million people every day.

Findus – imaginative frozen food since 1945

Originating in southern Sweden, the Findus brand grew out of a fruit cannery founded in 1905. In 1941 the business was renamed the Findus Canning Factory after it was purchased by the Freja Marabou confectionery company. Just four years later Findus broke into the fledgling Swedish frozen food market and by 1958 it was exporting to a number of different countries including the UK. Acquired by Nestlé in 1962, it adopted the distinctive Findus flag trademark in 1971.

As well as the standard frozen food range of fish fingers, beef burgers and cottage pies, Findus produced dishes that were quite imaginative for the time, including Crispy Pancakes, French Bread Pizzas and, perhaps most famously of all, Lean Cuisine, a selection of low-fat recipes which debuted in 1985 and was re-launched in 2000. In August 2015 the Findus Group's European operation was purchased by Nomad, the same concern that acquired Birds Eye earlier that year.

Jus-Rol – pastry made easy since 1954

Once, when anyone wanted to make a pie they had no option but to prepare their own pastry, so pastry-making was taught at school as part of the Domestic Science syllabus. All that changed when Tom Forsyth, a baker from Innerleithen in the Scottish Borders, invented pastry that could be bought ready to roll out. Choosing an admirably self-explanatory name for his product, he launched Jus-Rol in 1954 from premises in Coldstream, initially offering just puff and short crust pastry.

In 1959 rising demand for Jus-Rol necessitated a move from Coldstream to larger premises in Berwick-upon-Tweed. Here new lines were added to the Jus-Rol range including Yorkshire puddings, potato croquettes, apple strudels and sausage rolls. Overseas demand for the new products resulted in exports to Canada, the Middle East and Europe; in true coals to Newcastle fashion, Jus-Rol pizza dough was even exported to Italy.

Tom Forsyth died in 1971 but his business remained a family-run venture until it was acquired by the Grand Metropolitan Group towards the end of the Nineties. In 2001, Diageo (formerly Grand Metropolitan) sold Jus-Rol to General Mills. Known today as General Mills (Berwick) Ltd, Jus-Rol is the town's biggest employer.

Did you know...?

Jus-Rol's frozen Yorkshire puddings were served aboard the Royal Yacht *Britannia*.

Philadelphia – cool and creamy since 1872

Dairy farmers have been producing unripened soft white cheeses since the sixth century; Neufchatel, the best known variety, originated in the Normandy town of the same name where its manufacture is protected under EU law. However, a similar soft cheese has been produced in the USA for over 150 years, with those coming from the rich, fertile lands in the Philadelphia vicinity enjoying a particular reputation for excellence.

However, it was William Lawrence, a dairyman from Chester, a town in New York State located some 145 miles from Philadelphia, who invented cream cheese in 1872 by increasing the cream content in his soft cheese. For the first few years, sales of Lawrence's new product proved steady but unspectacular, a situation which changed in 1880 when it was discovered by a New York cheese broker called Alvah Reynolds. Reynolds came up with the idea of packing the cheese in foil wrappers and, with a winsome disregard for geographical accuracy, calling it Philadelphia Cream Cheese to instil confidence in its quality. It was a canny move; sales rocketed and Philadelphia Cream Cheese production expanded into other dairies in upstate New York. In 1903 the Philadelphia trademark was acquired by the Phenix (*sic*) Cheese Company of New York, followed by a merger in 1928 between Phenix and the Kraft Cheese Company from Chicago.

Philadelphia didn't arrive in the UK until 1960, with the first UK television ad airing in 1963. Since then many new varieties have been introduced, including full fat, medium fat, low fat, flavoured, and lactose free; there is even a variety that is blended with Cadbury's chocolate. Owned today by Mondelēz International, Philadelphia is available in more than eighty countries worldwide.

Primula – Norwegian for cheese since 1924

While many people will be familiar with Primula, the cheese that comes in a tube, far fewer few will be aware that its maker, the Kavli Group, has been ploughing its profits into good causes since the early Sixties. In fact, Kavli is owned by the Kavli Trust which exists solely to generate funds for good causes. This philanthropical state of affairs owes it origins to a decision made by Knut Kavli, son of company founder Olav Kavli who in 1893 started a cheese business in Norway when he was just 21. Travelling the world, Kavli senior succeeded in building up overseas demand for his cheeses and by 1924 hit on the idea of creating a long-lasting, spreadable cheese. He named it Primula after the flowers that herald the arrival of spring in his native land.

An important development came in 1929 when Kavli put his cheese spread into squeezable tubes. The UK's warm response to the innovation led to the establishment in 1936 of a Primula manufacturing operation near Newcastle. Having expanded several times, in 1962 the factory relocated to Gateshead where it remains today, producing 15 million tubes of cheese every year.

Olav Kavli died in 1958, leaving his son Knut in control of the business. Both father and son had always been committed to supporting worthwhile causes; now, with no offspring of his own to inherit from him in due course, Knut Kavli decided to take the philanthropy even further. In 1962 he established the Kavli Trust as sole owner of the Kavli business, with a legal requirement to donate profits to good causes such as humanitarian, research and cultural projects.

Did you know ... ?

There is money in squeezable cheese; as of 2015, even allowing for the profits they reinvest in the company's development, Kavli donate around £5 million annually to good causes.

Sara Lee – our just desserts since 1949

Charles Lubin epitomised the American Dream, rising from humble beginnings to found a global frozen foods business. His journey began in 1918 when, as a lad of 14, he was apprenticed to a Chicago baker. By 1935 he had gone into business with his brother-in-law, buying three neighbourhood bakeries called Community Bake Shops. As the venture prospered a further four shops were added to the chain but in 1949 Lubin and his brother-in-law went their separate ways. Now working alone, Lubin developed new products, the first of which was a cream cheesecake. Discussing possible names for the new confection, his wife jokingly suggested naming it after Sara Lee, their young daughter. Lubin liked the idea so much, he not only adopted the name for the cheesecake, he rebranded his entire business Kitchens of Sara Lee.

Up to this point Lubin's cakes were sold fresh but in 1952 a visitor from Texas sparked a change of direction. Impressed by the quality of the Sara Lee products, the man asked Lubin to ship them to Texas. This created a problem because fresh goods would perish before they reached their destination and Lubin knew that his recipes didn't freeze well. Undeterred, he reformulated his recipes without compromising on quality, and by 1955 was delivering them to forty-eight US states. Such was his success that just one year later Lubin was able to sell his business to Consolidated Foods for $2.8 million, at that time an enormous sum of money. Nevertheless, Lubin stayed on as Chief Executive Officer. He died in 1988.

Consolidated Foods – which was renamed the Sara Lee Corporation in 1985, at the same time that Kitchens of Sara Lee became Sara Lee Bakery – turned Lubin's enterprise into a global baked goods brand. In 2012, the Sara Lee Corporation was split in two, Hillshire Brands and D.E. Master Blenders, with Sara Lee frozen desserts belonging to the former.

Did you know...?

In 1989 Lubin's daughter, Sara Lee Schupf, appeared in television ads celebrating the brand's fortieth anniversary. Today she is a philanthropist and advocate of women in science.

Stork – marvellous marge since 1920

Margarine didn't exist until the latter half of the nineteenth century. It was invented in 1869 by French chemist Hyppolyte Mège-Mouriès in response to a call from Emperor Napoleon III for someone to create a butter substitute that his poorer subjects (and also his navy) could afford. Mège-Mouriès won the prize by churning beef fat with milk. Observing his invention's white lustre, Mège-Mouriès paused long enough to name it oleomargarine, from the Latin for oil and the Greek for pearly, before pocketing his prize money and selling his patent to Jurgens, a Dutch company with interests in the fat and soaps market. Within sixty years Jurgens would be part of Unilever.

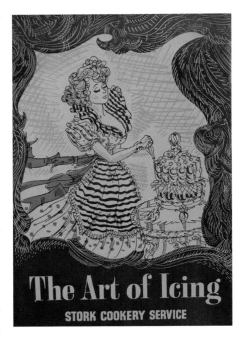

Meanwhile, improvements were made to the original margarine formula. Yellow food dye was added to it to make it look more like butter and in due course the beef fat was replaced by vegetable oils. Stork margarine made its debut in 1920 and by 1932 UK magazine adverts were extolling the product as a vital energy giver. A few years later the brand was sponsoring a show on Radio Lyons, an early commercial radio station. In 1939 the Stork Cookery Service was launched to help housewives stretch their wartime rations as far as possible. After the war Stork produced a number of new books featuring recipes made possible by the end of rationing, and in 1955 the product was one of the first brands to be advertised on ITV in its inaugural year. In the 1970s Stork soft tub margarine was introduced, followed by a series of adverts in which the late Leslie Crowther challenged members of the public to taste the difference between Stork and butter. Bruce Forsyth also featured in ads for the brand.

Did you know ... ?

In the US states of Vermont, New Hampshire and South Dakota, laws were once passed requiring margarine to be dyed pink; the strong dairy lobby feared the margarine industry and hoped the peculiar colour would have an adverse effect on it. The 'pink laws' were later overturned by the Supreme Court.

Stork is one of a number of products made at Unilever's margarine factory at Purfleet in Essex, a site that has existed since 1918 and is thought to be the largest margarine factory in the world.

Trex – light and easy since 1932

A home baking product derived from vegetable fat, Trex has been with us since the early Thirties although the roots of its original parent company stretch back to 1830. That was when one Edward Bibby bought the Conder Mill near Lancaster. By 1878 the mill was in the hands of Bibby's grandsons, Joseph and James Bibby, who as J. Bibby & Sons added a new line to their business by formulating and selling their own recipe of animal meal. When Conder Mill burned down in the 1880s, the operation moved to a new site at Fleet Square Mills. Nevertheless, their interests were prospering and the Bibbys were able to buy a second mill, this one situated in Liverpool to take advantage of the city's excellent trade links. A few years later they diversified into different markets including soap production and the crushing of oilseed, with the manufacture of compound cooking fats following in due course.

When Trex was launched in 1932 it was positioned as a dairy-free cooking fat, ideal for baking crisp pastry and light cakes. These qualities are still stressed today, along with the fact that Trex is lower in saturated fat than butter. J. Bibby & Sons was acquired by Princes Foods in 1968 which in turn was bought by the Mitsubishi Corporation in 1989.

Treat your family to TREX cooking

Trex gives pastry a tender lightness all its own, because it's already aerated when you buy it. This means easier rubbing-in as well as better eating. Use this pure, rich vegetable fat for lighter cakes too, and for crisp, digestible frying. You can make Trex Fruit Coronets every bit as good as the one above. Just follow the simple recipe shown here. *Remember, too, that there's a voucher on every Trex carton entitling you to a copy of the latest edition of Trex Cookery for 1/3d — half the normal price.*

TREX Fruit Coronets
8 oz. flour, S.R. or plain.
3½ oz. Trex.
¼ level teasp. salt.
3 tablesp. water.

Make pastry by rubbing-in method; roll out to ⅛" thickness, and cut with pastry wheel or knife into 4½" squares. Place squares centrally over inverted small moulds, press down the 4 points. Pinch pastry together between the points to fit the mould, or line ordinary patty tins and prick with a fork. Bake for 15-20 min. at 425°F. (Mark 7). Serve cold, filled with fruit, jelly and cream.

TREX
READY-AERATED
FOR
EXTRA LIGHTNESS

J. BIBBY & SONS, LTD.
LIVERPOOL 3

Did you know ... ?

Tubby Trex, the jolly baker featured for many years on all Trex advertising and packaging, was the mascot of the Trex Club. Prizes such as Tubby figurines and money boxes could be obtained by collecting jigsaw pieces printed on packets of Trex.

Wall's Ice Cream – a cool treat since 1922

From soft scoop vanilla to crunchy Cornettos, Wall's ice cream products are a part of our national consciousness. After all, there surely can't be a person in Britain over the age of 40 who doesn't know the first lines of the Cornetto song, sung to the tune of 'O Sole Mio'. What fans of the brand probably don't know, though, is that without Wall's sausages (see below) and other meat products, there would be no Wall's ice cream.

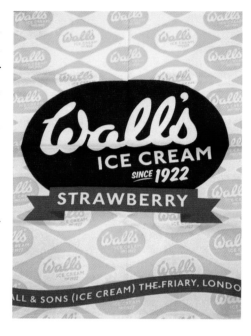

Already an established meat and pie company, Wall's first explored the idea of making ice cream in 1913. At the time the business tended to experience a sales slump during the summer months so diversifying into the ice cream market seemed a good idea. Before anything could happen, however, the First World War began and with the ensuing shortages it was 1922 before the proposal could be implemented. In the interim Wall's had been sold to Mac Fisheries and then on to Lever Brothers.

The first Wall's ice cream was sold in wrapped 'brickettes' alongside the regular meat products. When sales proved less than satisfactory, a young employee called Cecil Rodd mooted the idea of selling the ice cream from tricycles that trundled around the streets of London, emblazoned with the slogan 'Stop me and buy one'. This novel idea caught people's attention and once they had sampled the products – tubs and brickettes of ice cream, icy orange Sno Frutes and milky Sno Cremes – they came back for more. Meat experts Wall's had hit the big time with their ice cream sales.

The Cornetto, one of the brand's most popular products, was originally produced by Spica, an ice cream company from Naples; it was bought by Wall's in 1976 and launched in the UK around the same time. Wall's ice cream is now owned by Unilever.

Wall's Pork Sausages – great British bangers since 1786

Long before his grandson diversified into the ice cream business, Richard Wall set up a butcher's stall at St. James's Market in the heart of what is now London's West End. His good quality meat and tasty sausages brought him a roaring trade and by 1812 he was appointed 'Purveyor of Pork' to the Prince Regent. 1834 was a year of change for the Wall family, with a relocation of the business to premises in Jermyn Street followed by the death of Richard. For two years his widow Ann ran the concern with help from her son, Thomas, but on her death in 1836 he was left in sole control. Clearly a man possessed of good business acumen, young Wall continued to prosper and in due course he was joined by his two sons, another Thomas, and Frederick. Under Thomas II's leadership the business stepped up a gear; he took the company nationwide, opening a factory in Battersea to deal with the increased demand. Royal approval remained high during this time, with Queen Victoria, Edward VII and George V all bestowing their favour on the firm.

Thomas Wall II continued to run the family firm until his retirement in 1920, whereupon he sold it to Mac Fisheries which was owned by Lord Leverhulme and absorbed into Lever Brothers two years later. In 1929 Lever Brothers became part of Unilever which in 1994 sold the sausage and meat section of Wall's to the Irish Kerry Group.

Did you know ... ?

A noted philanthropist, in 1920 Thomas Wall II set up a Trust for the 'encouragement and assistance of education and social service'. He died in 1930 but the Thomas Wall Trust continues this work today.

Honourable mention: Country Life

Country Life butter was introduced in 1970 by a dairy trade consortium called the English Butter Marketing Company Ltd which grew out of the old Milk Marketing Board. Rebranded Dairy Crest in 1980, it was floated in 1996 and today is the leading British-owned dairy foods business.

SAUCES PICKLES

PRESERVES
AND
JELLIES

An exquisite and
poignant sauce for
which I'll say unto
my cook,—"There's
gold, go forth and be
a Knight!"

Ben Jonson

Chapter 5

Unbranded Generics

This chapter examines how some of our favourite unbranded food and drink items came by their names.

Battenberg cake

It is often said that this colourful, marzipan-wrapped sponge cake was first created in 1884 to mark the marriage of Princess Victoria, a granddaughter of Queen Victoria, to Prince Louis of Battenberg. The problem is that as yet no written evidence has been unearthed to support the story. However, the fact that the earliest known recipe for the cake was published in 1898, fourteen years after the date of the royal marriage, proves that it is at least plausible. Interestingly, it seems that the first incarnations of the
cake featured nine coloured panes of sponge. The reduction to four is thought to have occurred when Lyons launched their own version of the Battenberg sometime prior to the start of the Second World War.

Béchamel sauce

A white sauce made from butter, flour and milk, a Béchamel sauce is one of the cornerstones of classic French cuisine. Opinions differ as to how it came by its name but the most prevalent theory is that it was created in the seventeenth century by Pierre de la Varenne, a chef at the court of Louis XIV, and named in honour of an important courtier, the Marquis de Béchamel.

Beef Wellington

This popular mainstay of the banqueting menu may well have been created and named in honour of the first Duke of Wellington, victor of Waterloo and all-round military achiever. That's how the story goes and it would be wonderful if it were true. The trouble is that no evidence exists to link it to the Duke.

In fact, it turns out that Beef Wellington might actually be an American invention; certainly, Julia Child, the influential US cookery writer, was the first recorded person to use the term when she featured a recipe for 'filet of Beef Wellington' in a TV show broadcast in 1965. In essence, Child's recipe was a reworking of the classic French *boeuf en croute* with a new, Anglocentric name. The recipe caught on with the American public, found its way into *The White House Cookbook* of 1968 and eventually meandered across the Atlantic to appear in an English cookery book in 1970.

Bellini

A delicious blend of Prosecco and puréed white peaches, the cocktail known as a Bellini was invented in Venice in 1948 by Giuseppe Cipriani of Harry's Bar fame. Searching for something to call his new drink, Cipriani observed that its pretty pink colour was similar to a hue he had seen in the paintings of the Venetian Renaissance artist, Giovanni Bellini.

Bourbon (biscuit)

Consisting of chocolate buttercream sandwiched between two oblong layers of chocolate biscuit, the Bourbon has been a teatime favourite since its first appearance in 1910. Created by Peek Frean at their Bermondsey factory, it was initially named the Creola but in the 1930s it was changed to Bourbon. The reason is unknown but perhaps it was intended as a gesture of support for Alfonso XIII of Spain – a member of the royal house of Bourbon – who was ousted from his throne in 1931. It sounds unlikely but it is possible; after all, Peek Frean demonstrated good royalist tendencies when they baked a six-tier cake to mark the wedding of the future Queen Elizabeth II and Prince Philip in 1947. It wasn't the official wedding cake, though; that honour went to rival biscuiteers McVitie and Price who made the four-tier cake with ingredients given as a wedding present by the Australian Girl Guides. Nowadays there are many different versions of the biscuit available under the Bourbon name, including supermarket own-brands.

Bourbon (whiskey)

Brace yourselves because this one is contentious. To deal with the easy bit first, Bourbon is an American whiskey made primarily from corn. But where did it originate? Well, in Kentucky they say that it was first distilled there, in Bourbon County to be specific, hence the name. Yet the good folks of New Orleans tell a different tale. According to them, the home of Bourbon is Bourbon Street in their own fair city. The debate has been raging for decades and is no nearer resolution than when it started. However, on one thing both parties can agree: the name Bourbon is of French origin. Legend has it that the Kentuckians gave their county the name of the French king's family as a thank you for his support during the War of Independence. Bourbon Street in New Orleans, meanwhile, is named in honour of the Bourbon Duke of Orleans.

Wherever it originated, it's important to remember that Bourbon the drink is actually pronounced '*Burbon*'.

Caesar salad

Caesar salad was invented by restaurateur Caesar Cardini in Tijuana, Mexico in 1924. It was the Fourth of July and business had been so brisk that the restaurant was running out of food. Unwilling to turn away hungry customers, Cardini had a rummage in his kitchen and put together a salad from his few remaining supplies: romaine lettuce, garlic, croutons, Parmesan, hardboiled eggs, olive oil and Worcestershire sauce. With a natural showman's instinct, he prepared the salad at the table so the guests could watch the humble ingredients transform into something rather special. Proud of the dish he had created in less than ideal circumstances, Cardini decided to give it his first name, Caesar.

Chateaubriand

Chateaubriand is a mouth-watering beef fillet recipe created around 1822 by a French chef called Montmireil for his employer, the Vicomte de Chateaubriand, an author and a statesman. Its accompanying sauce is made from shallots, mushrooms, white wine and chicken stock.

Clementine

Oh my darling! A hybrid of a tangerine and an orange, the clementine is named after Clément Rodier, a French missionary who discovered the fruit in the garden of his orphanage in Algeria in 1902.

Coronation Chicken

When Queen Elizabeth II was crowned in 1953, palace officials were eager to offer visiting foreign dignitaries a tasty dish that required few ingredients and could be served cold. They had already commissioned society florist Constance Spry to look after the flowers at the coronation; now, knowing that Spry ran a domestic science school with her friend, an accomplished cook called Rosemary Hume, they commissioned the students at her school to provide the lunch. It was Hume who came up with the idea of chicken in a curried cream sauce with an accompanying rice salad. Dubbed Coronation Chicken, the dish proved a resounding success and to this day remains a buffet lunch regular.

Crêpes Suzette

This popular dessert consisting of pancakes (crêpes) flambéed at the table in sugar, orange juice and Grand Marnier was created by mistake. In 1895, young Henri Charpentier was working at the Cafe de Paris in Monte Carlo when he was called upon to serve HRH the Prince of Wales (later King Edward VII) and his friends. Just 14 years old at the time and understandably nervous, Henri bungled the crêpes he was preparing for his important customer. Working in front of a chafing dish, he allowed the entire dish to catch fire when he poured an alcohol-imbued sauce over the crêpes. Horrified, the lad flapped out the flames and then sampled the dish he had unintentionally flambéed. Much to his delight, it tasted wonderful so he served it to the Prince all the same. A famous gourmand, the Prince devoured the crêpes with evident relish and then demanded to know the name of the unfamiliar dish. Thinking fast, Charpentier named it Crêpes Princesse but HRH asked him to alter it to Crêpes Suzette in honour of the sole female dining with him. Wisely, Charpentier agreed and was rewarded the following day when the Prince gave him a jewelled ring, a panama hat and a cane.

The true identity of 'Suzette' remains a mystery. According to some sources, she was the daughter of one of the Prince's friends but others claim she was his paramour. Given his reputation as a Lothario, the latter seems more likely.

Dauphinoise potatoes

Sometimes also known as gratin dauphinois, this is a dish of sliced potatoes baked with milk, cream and cheese; delicious, but not for the weight-conscious. It originates from the Dauphiné region of France, hence the name. The earliest recorded serving of the dish was in 1788 at a dinner given by the Lieutenant-General of the Dauphiné.

Earl Grey

There is such a fog of speculation surrounding the origins of the bergamot-flavoured tea blend known as Earl Grey that those looking for the truth may as well consult the tea leaves. For decades it has been accepted that the Earl in question was the second Earl who served as Prime Minister from 1830 to 1834. That's certainly the story told at Howick Hall, the ancestral home of the Grey family. However, new research has come to light suggesting that it might be from his son, the third Earl (who was Secretary of State for War and the Colonies in the mid-nineteenth century) that the association stems.

Tracing the origins of that distinctive bergamot blend is equally problematic. At Howick, the story goes that the tea was blended by an obliging Chinese mandarin to suit the local water supply. Unfortunately the claim does not appear to be supported by documentary evidence. However, there is evidence to show that in the first half of the nineteenth century, bergamot was added to low-quality tea to disguise its short-

Did you know … ?

Bergamot oil is extracted from the rind of a variety of Seville orange known as a Bergamot.

comings. How this quick-fix for dodgy tea came to be associated with a superior, high-grade product enjoyed by the aristocracy remains anyone's guess, for the time being at least.

Eggs Benedict

Accounts differ as to the origins of this well-loved dish of poached eggs and ham (or sometimes smoked salmon), served on toasted muffins and then topped with hollandaise sauce. There are claims that it was created by Charles Ranhofer, the chef at Delmonico's in New York, sometime in the latter part of nineteenth century. According to this story, Ranhofer named the dish after a wealthy client called Mrs LeGrand Benedict.

The problem with this otherwise feasible story is that Mrs Beeton gave a recipe for 'Dutch sauce, for Benedict' in the first edition of her *Book of Household Management*. This was published in 1861 whereas Ranhofer's recipe was not published until 1894. Muddying the waters further is the evidence offered by Elizabeth David in her seminal cookery book, *French Provincial Cooking*. According to Ms. David, '*oeufs bénédictine*' is a traditional French dish consisting of pureed salt cod and potatoes spread on fried bread before being topped with poached eggs and hollandaise sauce.

Taking all accounts into consideration, it seems likely that Eggs Benedict originated in France, although the first recipe was substantially different to the one we know today. Over time it has been tweaked to increase its appeal to a wider audience. Additionally, the word 'Benedict' and the fact that the original recipe used eggs and salt cod, suggests the dish may have been eaten at Lent by the monks of the Benedictine order.

Garibaldi biscuits

Giuseppe Garibaldi was an Italian general who played a pivotal role in his country's struggle for independence. Quite how he came to share his name with a rectangular, currant-filled biscuit of British origin is not immediately apparent, although one rather unedifying theory does exist, of which more in due course.

First, though, to the biscuit itself: created in 1861 by Jonathan Carr for the London-based Peak Frean company, it consists of two layers of crisp biscuit with a sweet currant filling that doesn't quite relieve the dryness of the baked dough. It is the appearance of the currants that has given the Garibaldi its nickname of squashed fly biscuit. Difficult to enjoy without a drink, it comes into its own when consumed with a cup of tea.

As for the link between Giuseppe Garibaldi and his biscuit namesake, it is said that during one of his campaigns, supplies had run so low that he was unable to feed his men. Undeterred, he instructed them to soak slices of bread in horse blood, adding foraged berries to the resulting mush. While the story may be true, it seems unlikely that a commercial organisation would choose to name a new product after this unpleasant-sounding concoction. However, Garibaldi was riding high in British public opinion in 1861 following some daring exploits the previous year. It therefore seems probable that Peak Frean simply chose to name their new biscuit after a popular personality of the day. Rival biscuit companies soon produced their own versions which they also called Garibaldis since the name was not protected by trademark.

John Dory

While the John Dory may not be the most attractive fish, its white flesh is boneless, firm and full of flavour. Found in European waters, it is known as St. Pierre in France, apparently due to a legend concerning St Peter who is said to have given the fish its distinctive black spot when he pressed his thumb to its side.

Interestingly, the French are indirectly responsible for the English name which is believed to be a distortion of '*jaune dorée*', meaning golden yellow (the natural colour of the fish). Since there is an ancient Cornish folksong called 'John Dory', it is easy to understand how the unfamiliar French phrase was transmuted into something comfortably recognisable.

Macadamia nut

Originally called 'jindilli' or 'boombera' (depending on location) by the indigenous population of Australia, the macadamia nut was renamed in honour of Scottish-born chemist John McAdam in the mid-nineteenth century. Before then, the nut's extremely hard shell had deterred the European settlers from sampling it but once they had worked out that a swift bash with a hammer would do the trick, its popularity slowly grew. By 1858 it had become sufficiently important for leading botanist Ferdinand von Mueller to deem it worthy of a new name. In honour of his good friend, the Scottish-born chemist John MacAdam, he dubbed the nut the macadamia.

History has not recorded the aboriginals' opinion of the new name.

Mandarin (see also Tangerine)

Question: When is a mandarin not a mandarin? *Answer:* When it's a tangerine.

Or, to put it more plainly, the only real difference between a mandarin and a tangerine is the name. In all other respects, they are the same fruit, *Citrus reticulate Blanco*.

The 'mandarin' moniker came about because people thought they came from China whereas the 'tangerine' indicates a belief that the tasty little fruit originated in Tangier. There is a germ of truth in both theories; the fruit was first grown in the south of China and was exported to the western world via the port of Tangier.

Margarita

While it is believed that the Margarita, a cocktail made from tequila, Cointreau and lime juice may have been tickling the taste buds of thirsty customers since as far back as the 1920s, nobody seems sure how it came by its name. According to one account it was named after Dallas socialite Margaret Sames who 'invented' the drink in 1948. The problem here is that the cocktail was being advertised as a Margarita as early as 1945. Other stories cite various different Margarets, Marjories and Margaritas as the inspiration for the cocktail, including one Margarita Cansino who became better known to the world as the screen star Rita Hayworth.

With no definitive proof for any of these theories, it's worth considering a completely different origin for the name. During the early years of the twentieth century there was a very popular cocktail called the Daisy which was made by blending brandy and citrus. It seems plausible that whenever tequila, a drink from Spanish-speaking Mexico, was used to make the cocktail, the name would change to Margarita, the Spanish word for daisy.

Mayonnaise

The recipe for this ubiquitous sauce is believed to come from the Menorcan town of Mahón. Thus it is of Spanish origin although the word 'mayonnaise' is French. In Spain, however, it was known originally as '*salsa mahonesa*' and the Catalans still call it '*maonesa*' to this day. While nobody knows the exact date mayonnaise was invented, its first mention in the English language appears to be in the 1823 journal of Irish beauty and novelist Lady Blessington.

The Mahón story is widely accepted everywhere except in France. There, some claim it as a French invention although opinions differ as to the details. One theory is that mayonnaise is a corruption of '*moyeunaise*', a term derived from the ancient French word for egg yolk. Another is that it was named after the Duke of Mayenne while a third claims it was invented in the French town of Bayonne but for reasons unknown, over the course of time the letter M replaced the B.

Melba toast

See Peach Melba

Mulligatawny

This spicy Indian soup was brought to Britain by soldiers, civil servants, teachers and missionaries returning from the Raj. The name comes from the Tamil expression '*milagu tani*' which translates as 'pepper water'. Truly authentic versions are vegetarian but meat varieties were created to cater for Western preferences. While recipes for mulligatawny have been appearing in British cookery books since the nineteenth century, most people will only know the canned version produced by Heinz.

Pavlova

A light and airy dessert consisting of meringue, fruit and whipped cream, Pavlova was created when Anna Pavlova, the legendary Russian prima ballerina, visited the

Southern Hemisphere in the 1920s. The meringue was said to represent the dancer's tutu, the cream her frothy net underskirt and the fruit – originally sliced kiwis – the green cabbage roses that decorated her tutu.

So much is universally agreed upon although, in Australia and New Zealand at least, that's where the agreement stops. The Australians claim the recipe was created in 1935 by Bert Sachse, a chef from Perth, Western Australia. In New Zealand, the counter-claim is that they were publishing recipes for Pavlova in 1928, seven years before Mr Sachse's alleged invention.

In 2010, the *Oxford English Dictionary* (*OED*) appeared to come out in support of the Kiwis' claim when it credited New Zealand with publishing the first Pavlova recipe. Having provided this useful clarification, it immediately muddied the waters again by giving the origin of the dessert as Australia <u>and</u> New Zealand. So that's settled, then.

Peach Melba

The craze for creating and naming dishes in honour of prominent celebrities has pretty much died out today (Mussels Minogue, anyone, or how about a Caramel Clooney?) but back in the nineteenth century, leading chefs enhanced their reputations by doing precisely that. So perhaps it's not altogether surprising that one of the best-loved personalities of the late nineteenth century, the Australian opera singer Dame Nellie Melba, had no fewer than four concoctions named after her.

The man responsible for all four creations was Auguste Escoffier, the renowned chef at The Savoy in London where the singer was a regular customer. While neither Melba garniture (a dish of sauce-covered tomatoes stuffed with chicken, mushrooms and truffles), nor Melba sauce (a purée of redcurrants and raspberries) are often found on modern menus, two of Escoffier's Melba concepts do live on today. The first, the thin and crunchy Melba toast, can be used as a substitute for crackers and is sometimes given to invalids. More delicious by far, however, is the glorious concoction of ice cream, poached peaches and raspberry sauce known to grateful diners the world over as Peach Melba.

Did you know...?

Dame Nellie Melba was born Helen Porter Mitchell. She chose Nellie Melba as a stage name in order to pay tribute to Melbourne, a city she loved.

Sandwich

Picture the scene, if you will. It is London in the eighteenth century; the hour is late and his stomach is rumbling but John Montagu, the gambling-addicted fourth Earl of Sandwich, is reluctant to leave the gaming table. He's had a good run with the cards and fears his luck will change if he takes a break. His solution? Searching his memory, he recalls dishes served to him during his travels in the Mediterranean, exotic mouthfuls of flat breads stuffed with meat and interesting vegetables. These tasty morsels lend themselves to being eaten one-handed, the hungry Earl remembers.

Summoning a valet, he sends orders to his surprised kitchen staff for a meal of roast beef encased between two pieces of bread, staples which no self-respecting English cook would dream of being without. The food arrives, the aristocratic hunger is appeased and the gaming continues unabated. Full of admiration, the Earl's gambling cronies hurry home and instruct their own staff to serve similar fare whenever they are gambling – which, this being the eighteenth century, is often. Thus the humble sandwich is born.

Satsuma

The satsuma is a seedless, easy-to-peel variety of mandarin originating in China and Japan. It is named after the Satsuma region of Japan from which the fruits were first exported to Europe.

Did you know ... ?

The name Satsuma also applies to a type of distinctive Japanese pottery. Made all over Japan, it is called Satsuma because, as with the fruit, it was from here that the pottery was exported.

Sole Véronique

It was our old friend Auguste Escoffier (see also Peach Melba) who devised this dish of Dover sole poached in dry white wine and then covered in a sauce made by combining the poaching liquor with cream and grapes. Having moved on from The Savoy, Escoffier was working at the Carlton Hotel in London in 1904 when Véronique, an acclaimed operetta by André Messager, opened at the Apollo Theatre. With theatre-goers going wild for Véronique, wily Escoffier cashed in on its success by naming his tasty new fish supper in its honour.

Tangerine

See Mandarin.

Tarte Tatin

Legend has it that tarte Tatin, a delicious confection of caramelised apples cooked upside-down in pastry, was created by happy accident. The story goes something like this: at the end of the nineteenth century, sisters Fanny (real name Stéphanie) and Caroline Tatin were running a hotel in the town of Lamotte-Beuvron in France. One day Fanny – who was responsible for the cooking – left some apples she was simmering in sugar and butter on the stove too long and as a result they caramelised.  In an attempt to recover the dish, she popped a lid of pastry on top of the apples and thrust the pan into the oven to bake. Full of trepidation, she served the dessert to her hungry guests and was immensely relieved when they liked it so much they came back for more.

It should be noted that culinary killjoys like to pick holes in the story, pointing out that similar recipes were being enjoyed in that region of France long before Fanny Tatin caramelised her apples. Nevertheless, it was the Tatins who popularised the dish and gave it a name that is recognised worldwide.

Tom Collins

As we have already seen, things are rarely clear cut when it comes to finding out how a recipe or type of drink came by its name. In the case of the etymology of the Tom Collins cocktail, however, there is more than the usual level of confusion and misinformation but, having sifted through the various accounts, the following would seem to be the truth.

In London in the late eighteenth century, a waiter called John Collins served alcoholic drinks to the young ne'er-do-wells who frequented a Mayfair drinking establishment called Limmer's Old House. Such was the renown of Mr Collins that a gin-based long drink was named after him. Fast forward around seventy years to 1869 when a recipe for a John Collins was published, specifying the use of a gin brand called Old Tom together with the other ingredients (soda, lemon and sugar). With John Collins of Limmer's fading from public memory, the drink became known as a Tom Collins because of the Old Tom gin.

That's where the story would end, were it not for the 'Great Tom Collins Hoax of 1874'. In a nutshell, in New York that year some wag began a craze for telling unsuspecting people that a chap by the name of Tom Collins was spreading nasty rumours about them. Anyone gullible enough to fall for it would immediately storm off in search of this fellow Tom Collins in order to put a stop to the slander, unaware that he didn't exist and that it was all a mighty joke. The hoax was widely reported in the press, leading some to believe that it was the inspiration for the Tom Collins cocktail.

Tournedos Rossini

A luxurious dish of fillet steak served on toasted bread and then topped with foie gras, Tournedos Rossini was considered the epitome of gastronomic sophistication several decades ago and, like many retro dishes, it is enjoying a resurgence in popularity today.

The dish was created and named for Gioachino Rossini, the famous Italian composer responsible for *The Barber of Seville* and *William Tell*, by Casimir Moissons, the chef at the Maison Doreé in Paris which Rossini frequented on a regular basis.

Victoria Sandwich (aka Victoria Sponge)

A sweet, diet-destroying enticement of two sponge layers sandwiched together with jam and cream (or buttercream), the Victoria sandwich cake reigns supreme over the British tea table, much as the monarch for whom it is named reigned over Britain and the Empire for nearly sixty-four years. In fact, during Queen Victoria's lengthy reign, it was quite the fashion to name things after her, hence the plethora of Victoria provinces, towns, parks and buildings to be found worldwide today. The craze extended to food items, too, although today most of the edible Victorias have been forgotten, with the notable exceptions of the plum and the cake.

While there seems to be no definitive evidence that Queen Victoria regularly partook of 'her' cake, it seems probable that she would have consumed the odd teatime slice given that Isabella Beeton published a recipe for Victoria Sandwiches in her 1861 *Book of Household Management*. That, incidentally, was the year that the Queen's beloved husband, Prince Albert, died. Perhaps the grieving widow found consolation in cake.

Waldorf salad

Remember the scene in *Fawlty Towers* in which an American guest asks Basil Fawlty for a Waldorf salad?

> Customer: 'Could you make me a Waldorf salad?'
> Fawlty: 'I think we're just out of Waldorfs.'

Poor Basil! If only he had known that the Waldorf is a salad of celery, apples and mayonnaise served on a bed of lettuce, sometimes with the addition of walnuts.

It was created in 1896 at the famous Waldorf-Astoria Hotel in New York by Oscar Tschirky, the maître d'hôtel, and served to 1,500 members of the social elite. The dish was a tremendous success with the guests and immediately became the must-serve salad for the socially ambitious.

Part II

House & Home

Chapter 6

Appliances, Gadgets and Everyday Consumables

If you have ever stopped to reflect on how difficult life must have been before the invention of our most useful household gadgets and gizmos, this section is for you. From sleek appliances that dent the bank balance to disposable items costing a few pounds at most, the brands featured here are ones that we have come to rely upon. And with a few indulgent exceptions – notably AGA and Jacuzzi – they are our reliable work-horses, the tools and trappings of everyday domestic life. Some, especially inexpensive consumables such as Sellotape and Velcro, we take for granted even though we know deep down that managing without them would be unthinkable. To others we give our gratitude for making our household chores immeasurably easier or we would if we were ever able to pause long enough to consider them. So given that modern life is fast and busy, and that these products enable most of us to keep up with it, now seems as good an opportunity as ever to reflect on the brands that keep British home life ticking over.

AGA Range Cookers – cosy and covetable since 1922

Invented by a Swedish Nobel prize-winner before being appropriated by the British middle classes, the AGA is more than just a highly functional household appliance; it is a statement of aspirational intent. It was in 1912 that ingenious engineer Dr Gustaf Dalén was awarded the Nobel Prize for Physics. Sadly that same year he lost his sight whilst conducting safety tests on acetylene cylinders. He was at home convalescing from this horrific injury, the story goes, when he became frustrated by the inefficiency of his kitchen range which required constant attention in order to prevent it from going out. Undaunted by his blindness, Dalén felt inspired to create something better and by 1922 he had produced the AGA, a mighty cast-iron cooker with two ovens and two large hotplates.

By 1929 a British firm had acquired the licence to manufacture the AGAs in Smethwick. Sales were boosted by the talents of one David Ogilvy who later co-founded the famous Ogilvy & Mather advertising firm agency. According to the agency's website, 'Ogilvy's career with AGA Cookers was astonishing. He sold stoves to nuns, drunkards, and everyone in between.'

The Second World War led to an increase in orders as the Government bought AGAs for use in the canteens of munitions factories and hospitals. At one point demand was so high that there was a waiting time of twenty-seven weeks, so a new plant was opened in Shropshire. In 1947 virtually all the manufacturing moved to the Coalbrookdale foundry, famous for being the birthplace of the Industrial Revolution. Both the AGA and the Rayburn, the British-invented cooker-cum-water heater introduced in the 1940s, are still produced in Coalbrookdale to this day.

Originally the AGA was produced with a cream paint finish but in 1956 models were introduced in pale blue, pale green and white. A more radical innovation occurred in the Sixties when a fall in the popularity of solid fuels saw the introduction of oil- and gas-fired cookers. Around the same time the colour choices were extended to include dark blue, red, yellow and black. The AGAs grew in popularity throughout the Eighties and Nineties, with spreads in lifestyle magazines showing covetable kitchens complete with AGA and sleeping Labradors.

Although there has been a strong trend for industrial-style kitchens of late, AGAs have retained their popularity. According to one survey, a house with an AGA will sell more quickly than one without and, while buying one is a significant investment, the cost is recouped when the house is sold.

Did you know ... ?

First coined in 1992 by Terence Blacker writing in *Publishing News*, an 'AGA saga' is a genre of contemporary fiction set in 'middle England', ownership of an AGA apparently epitomising the prosperous, country-loving people whose lives form the backdrop to the novels.

Arthur Price – cutting-edge cutlery since 1902

Originating in Birmingham in 1902, Arthur Price is a family-owned cutlery company currently run by Simon Price, the great-grandson of the eponymous founder. Over the years a reputation for quality craftsmanship has brought the firm two Royal Warrants and a slew of well-known customers.

Founding father Arthur Price spent twenty years learning the flatware trade before he set up his own small operation in the Aston area of Birmingham. It was a competitive marketplace but Price's skill, hard work and sound business sense ensured success. This was underlined in 1912 when the firm was commissioned to supply a premium range of cutlery for the ill-fated *Titanic*. The design was recreated in 2012 to commemorate the ship's centenary.

The firm demonstrated its commitment to innovation when it became the first to make spoons and forks from chromium plate and by the 1950s it had become the country's largest manufacturer of stainless steel cutlery. Today the business's headquarters are in Staffordshire but it has factories in Birmingham and Sheffield, historic centres of cutlery and flatware production.

Biro – spatter-free writing since 1938

The Biro is a classic example of a registered trademark that has become genericised i.e. one that is used as a synonym for all similar products regardless of brand. Strictly speaking the correct term for such a pen is a ballpoint but in many English-speaking countries, the UK included, 'biro' with a lower-case 'b' is used instead.

The Biro story began in Hungary in the 1930s when a Hungarian-Jewish journalist called László Biró grew impatient with the fountain pen's tendency to leak ink. Determined to develop a reliable alternative, he embarked on a series of experiments with help from his brother George. Eventually he devised a pen tipped with a metal ball bearing that used a pressurised tube and capillary action to draw ink through the rotating ball.

Biró patented his invention in 1938 before fleeing Hungary to avoid persecution. Settling in Argentina, he and his brother set about producing their pens. Their first significant business came from the RAF which, impressed by the pen's ability to write at high altitude without leakage, placed an order for 30,000 units. It was not long after this that Biró sold his patent to Marcel Bich, founder of the Société Bic company which introduced the bestselling BIC Cristal ballpoint in 1950. László Biró continued to live in Argentina until his death in 1985. He is remembered there every year when Argentinian Inventors Day is celebrated on his birthday, 29 September.

Denby Stoneware – made of strong stuff since 1809

Believed to be the top tableware choice for UK brides, Denby has been gracing our kitchens for over 200 years. It all began in 1806 when an extensive seam of clay was discovered in Denby in Derbyshire during the construction of a new road. Three years later William Bourne, a pottery manufacturer from nearby Belper, set up a small salt-glazed pottery on the site, putting his son Joseph in charge of the operation. Initially production was limited to hardwearing stoneware bottles which were widely used in the nineteenth century as a cheaper alternative to glass.

During his tenure at Denby Joseph Bourne patented many innovative techniques for firing salt-glazed stoneware, and established a reputation for the quality of his firm's output. He was succeeded in 1860 by his son, Joseph Harvey Bourne, but following the latter's death just nine years later it fell to his widow, Sarah, to take over. She proved herself more than capable, keeping the company prosperous and adding new lines including Artware, new types of kitchenware and the unglamorous-sounding but highly necessary telegraphic insulators.

In the 1920s Denby, by now a limited company run by Joseph Harvey Bourne's nephew, was making two distinct product lines: functional kitchenware such as jelly moulds, pie dishes and hot water bottles; and decorative home wares such as bowls and vases which were stamped Danesby Ware to differentiate them from the more prosaic output. Now that salt-glazed products had fallen out of favour, Denby developed new firing techniques to create kitchenware lines that were destined to become long-running favourites. At the same time they diversified into the production of animal figurines which have become hugely popular with collectors.

During the Second World War Denby was obliged to restrict tableware production to 'Utility Brown' but once the war was over exciting new designs introduced by Glyn Colledge and others became best-sellers. This success was cemented in the 1970s by Denby's introduction of oven-to-tableware – essentially items that were robust enough to withstand the oven and good looking enough to put on the table. As for today, modern Denby stoneware is safe to use in the oven, dishwasher, microwave and freezer. Quality and reputation remains such a cornerstone of the business that every piece passes thought twenty-five pairs of hands before being passed fit for sale. Having remained a family business until 1942, Denby is now owned by Valco Capital Partners.

Did you know … ?

It is alleged that four upturned Denby mugs can hold the weight of a double-decker bus.

Hoover – keeping dirt at bay since 1908

The Hoover brand name has become so familiar that it is now used generically to describe any kind of dust guzzler. Yet it might so easily have been the 'spangler' that became synonymous with the vacuum cleaner instead of the 'hoover'.

It was in the early years of the twentieth century that James M. Spangler, an asthmatic department store janitor from Canton, Ohio invented a device he called a suction sweeper to help minimise his exposure to dust. Having patented his invention in 1907, Spangler sold the patent the following year to his cousin's husband, one

William Henry Hoover. Working in partnership with Spangler, Hoover established the Electric Suction Sweeper Company and began producing and marketing the new invention. It was here that Hoover's business acumen came in handy. Having advertised the product, rather than dealing directly with interested customers he chose to sell via reputable stores that earned commission from each sale, thereby laying the groundwork for an impressive dealer network. At the same time the company continued to work on designs for better, more technologically-advanced cleaning devices.

The business – which took the Hoover name in 1922 – arrived in the UK in 1918. The British Vacuum Cleaner and Engineering Company had been in existence since 1902 but Hoover was soon outselling them. Even so, vacuum cleaners remained beyond the reach of most ordinary British people until the arrival of Hoover's Constellation in 1952. This pioneering design remained in production until 1975.

Hoover vacuum cleaners have come a very long way since the early days of the suction sweeper. Bagless, cordless and now even person-less since the arrival of the robot cleaner, they have revolutionised our ability to keep our homes clean. Surely poor asthmatic James Spangler would be impressed and also a little bit envious. The company he co-founded, meanwhile, is now owned in Europe by Candy and in the USA by Techtronic Industries.

Did you know … ?

The old Hoover factory in Perivale on the outskirts of London was awarded Grade II listed status in 1980 on account of its fabulous Art Deco exterior; it is now a branch of Tesco.

Jacuzzi – hydrotherapy heaven since 1956

Long before it became synonymous with whirlpool baths, the Jacuzzi name was associated with the aircraft that carried the US mail. The story began at the start of the twentieth century when the seven Jacuzzi brothers left their farm in Casarsa, northern Italy and emigrated to America. Blessed with inventive capabilities, in 1915 they invested in a machine shop and created a propeller that was used on military planes. They later invented a high-wing monoplane with enclosed cabin which was used by the US Postal Service, and became the go-to people in the agricultural pump industry.

It was their expertise in the latter area that led to their most famous invention, although it took a family health problem to bring it about. When Kenneth, son of Candido Jacuzzi, was diagnosed with rheumatoid arthritis in the 1940s, hydrotherapy treatment was found to be beneficial. The trouble was that Kenneth had to attend hospital to receive the treatment so the family set their best brains to inventing a home solution. The hydrotherapy pump they came up with gradually established a small niche in the surgical supplies market but the big development came in 1968 when Roy Jacuzzi invented the 'Roman Bath', the first fully-integrated whirlpool bath.

Jacuzzi remained a family concern until 1979; since then, ownership has changed several times and at the time of writing it is owned by Apollo Management, a private equity firm.

Did you know ... ?

One of the original Jacuzzi brothers opened a vineyard in California's Sonoma Valley in the 1920s; still producing wine today, it uses a propeller logo recalling the company's first product.

Kenwood Chef – kitchen wizardry since 1950

Launched at the Ideal Home Exhibition of 1950, the first Kenwood Chef (model A700) offered a heady mix of glamour and convenience to women long accustomed to making do with dreary utility wares and labour-intensive tools. Every bride wanted to own one so it's not surprising that when it first appeared in Harrods it sold out within a week. Food preparation would never be the same again.

The man behind the Kenwood Chef was Kenneth Wood, a former electrical engineer with the RAF who in 1947 founded a company in Woking. With a working capital of £800 he took on around twenty members of staff and began producing kitchen appliances. His first offering was a toaster, shortly followed by a food mixer known as the A200. However, it was the arrival of the multi-functional Kenwood Chef in 1950 that projected his company into the stratosphere, turning Wood into one of the UK's youngest millionaires by the time he was 38.

By 1962 the firm had outgrown the Woking premises and relocated to a new and highly advanced manufacturing site in Havant, Hampshire. During that decade an updated version of the Kenwood Chef was introduced, costing the not insignificant sum of 30 guineas. In 1968 Kenwood was taken over by Thorn Electrical Industries Ltd. Today it is owned by De'Longhi, having been acquired by the Italian manufacturer in 2001. Kenneth Wood died in 1997, fifty years after founding the company that still bears his name. The Kenwood Chef, his best-loved invention, remains a popular choice despite strong competition from other brands, although it is no longer manufactured in the UK.

Did you know … ?

A Kenwood Chef advertisement from 1961 carried the questionable slogan: 'The Chef does everything but cook - that's what wives are for!'

Parker Pens – better writing since 1888

Poorly-made pens that leaked ink everywhere were the bane of George Safford Parker's life. The Wisconsin-born telegraphy teacher made a little extra income by selling pens for the John Holland Pen Company, a pioneer of the fountain pen industry. Unfortunately, the pens were often faulty and Parker found himself fixing them out of a sense of moral obligation. After a while, the thought occurred to him that he could probably create a more reliable pen and thus in 1888, at the age of 25, he founded the Parker Pen Company in Janesville, Wisconsin.

Having patented his first fountain pen in 1889, he experienced a major breakthrough in 1894 with the introduction of the Lucky Curve ink feed system, a revolutionary system which significantly reduced the occurrence of ink leakage. Another important development was the Parker Trench Pen which had small black pellets contained in its barrel; when combined with water, the pellets created around half a pint of ink. Of particular interest to the military, the Trench Pen earned Parker an important contract with the US War Department. This success was enlarged on in 1921 with the launch of the Parker Duofold, widely regarded as one of the most iconic pens ever made. George S. Parker remained as president of the company until 1933 and died in 1937. Parker Pens arrived in the UK in 1945 with the acquisition of the long-established Valentine Pen Factory in Newhaven. The firm was awarded a Royal Warrant in 1962 as sole supplier to the Royal Household of pens, pencils and inks.

Acquired by Gillette in 1993, the Parker Pen Co was then sold in 2000 to Newell Rubbermaid, the American consumer products titan based in Atlanta.

Price's Patent Candles – burning brightly since 1830

Unlike many of the brands featured in this book, Price's Patent Candle Company was not named after its founder, nor was that founder an ambitious young man intent on making his way in the world. Instead, the company was set up by William Wilson, a 58-year-old Scotsman based in London who was already successful as an importer of Russian merchandise. An astute businessman, Wilson had identified an opportunity in the candle market which currently offered no middle ground between dirty tallow candles at the cheap end of the spectrum and those made from beeswax which were highly priced.

Rising to the challenge, in 1830 Wilson and his partner Benjamin Lancaster established premises in South London and set about making clean, mid-priced candles using coconut fats sourced from their own 1,000-acre coconut plantation in Ceylon. Unwilling to put their names to the endeavour, they dubbed it Edward Price & Co even though there was no Edward Price, changing the name to Price's Patent Candle Company in 1847. Candles made from palm oil cleaned with sulphuric acid came next, an astute move which for complex political reasons found favour with many.

By now a successful concern, Price's embarked on a programme of acquisitions and expansion, most notably opening a factory near Birkenhead which enabled it to double its imports of palm oil. By 1855 the company was employing 2,300 people, around half of whom were boys who enjoyed better than average working conditions thanks to the progressive beliefs of the deeply religious Wilson family. Their benevolence was demonstrated in other ways, too, such as the construction of model housing in Liverpool, free schooling for the youngsters and the introduction of profit sharing and contributory pensions for all.

Having kept pace with some radical advances in candle production, by the start of the twentieth century Price's was the largest candle manufacturer in the world. In 1919 the firm was taken over by Lever Brothers, the soap leviathan which occupied neighbouring Merseyside premises. Since then the business has endured its ups and downs and ownership has changed hands a number of times. In 2003 it was acquired by SER Wax Industry, an Italian company which is Europe's leading manufacturer of raw wax materials. However, Price's UK operations are based in Bedford.

Did you know ... ?

As holders of the Queen's Royal Warrant, Price's supply candles for all royal state occasions including coronations, weddings, lying-in-states and funerals. The first state occasion at which Price's candles were used was the Duke of Wellington's funeral in 1852.

Pyrex – handling the hot stuff since 1915

Having used Pyrex products in our kitchens for generations, we might struggle to appreciate quite how miraculous the heat-withstanding, oven-proof glassware once seemed to housewives all too accustomed to casseroles cracking in the oven. In fact, the inspiration for Pyrex is often attributed to one such woman, Bessie Littleton, the wife of a scientist working at Corning Glass Works in New York State. For several years Mr Littleton had been developing Nonex, a glass able to withstand extreme temperatures, for use in railway lanterns. Nonex went into production in 1909 and a few years later Mrs Littleton, exasperated with her unreliable ovenware, decided to conduct an experiment of her own. Using a specially adapted piece of Nonex she baked a sponge cake and found the result highly satisfactory. The bigwigs at Corning took note and in 1915 the first twelve pieces of Pyrex were offered for sale by the firm's new consumer products division.

This miracle glassware came to the UK in 1922 when James A. Jobling and Co of the Wear Flint Glass Works in Sunderland acquired Empire-wide rights to manufacture and distribute Pyrex. Practical, reliable and easy to care for, it quickly won over British housewives, many of whom found themselves cooking for their families for the first time due to the scarcity of domestic servants. Sales rocketed and at its apogee the Sunderland site was employing around 3,000 people. Sadly for the area, it was not destined to last. Corning acquired Joblings in 1973, changing the firm's name to Corning Ltd two years later. In 2007 production moved to France and the Sunderland factory was closed.

Did you know ... ?

Vintage (i.e. second-hand) Pyrex is widely collected today by kitchen enthusiasts; all types are collected although by far the most popular is coloured Pyrexware which was introduced in 1947.

Roberts Radio – tuning us in since 1932

In recent years the much-loved Roberts Radio has experienced something of a renaissance thanks to its classic good looks and consistent reliability. Yet it hasn't always been plain sailing for the company which was started in 1932 by two young men eager to work for themselves.

Londoners Harry Roberts and Leslie Bidmead were both working in the fledgling wireless industry when they met and decided to go into business together. With £50 start-up capital, some of which came from the sale of Bidmead's motorbike, they took premises near Oxford Circus and started to create top-quality radios. At first their output was just three radios per week, with Bidmead concentrating on production and Roberts handling sales. A major breakthrough came when the Harrods' radio buyer ordered half a dozen sets. When other department stores followed suit, Roberts and Bidmead knew their company had a future.

The company holds two Royal Warrants and in fact the Royal Family were early admirers of the Roberts radio. In 1939 Princess Elizabeth, the future Queen, was given one by her mother, Queen Elizabeth, as a birthday present. The following year the Queen bought the Roberts Model M4D for her personal use.

Having outgrown its premises several times already, in 1962 the company moved to a purpose-built factory in West Molesey, Surrey. This is where the iconic Model RT1 was produced in 1958, its design inspired by a handbag owned by Elsie Roberts, Harry's wife. Competition from the Far East led to challenging times during the Seventies and Eighties but the firm's fortunes were revived in the Nineties when one of its radios featured in a Martini ad, sparking an influx of requests. The RT1 was promptly re-issued in its original design and has since been produced in a wide variety of colours and patterns.

Despite the strong retro trend, the company also has a range of ultra-modern radios and iPod docks. In 1999 it produced the world's first portable DAB radio and during the first years of the twenty-first century started selling BBC World Service branded wide-band radio sets. Acquired in 1994 by Glen Dimplex, the Irish electrical goods firm, Roberts Radio is now based in Mexborough, South Yorkshire,

Salter Scales – taking the weight since 1760

In 1760 two mechanically-minded brothers embarked on a small-scale manufacturing venture that was destined to grow beyond their wildest expectations, thereby ensuring that their name would still be known over 250 years later. Richard and William Salter had a humble start, making springs and pocket steelyards (spring balances) from their cottage in Bilston in the Black Country. In 1770 they relocated their successful enterprise to the nearby town of West Bromwich where it soon became a major employer. During the 1790s the firm was run by William Salter's sons, John and George, but following his brother's death in 1824, George took sole control and the company's name was changed to George Salter & Co.

As it progressed, the company widened its portfolio of products to include irons, roasting jacks and even musket bayonets as well as many different kinds of domestic weighing scales. Salter made Britain's first bathroom scales and in 1895 created the first English typewriter. The firm became a limited company in 1915 and by 1950 it had in excess of 2,000 employees. Acquired by Staveley Industries in 1972, it was split into separate product-determined subsidiaries but following a couple of management buy-outs, Salter Housewares was bought in 2004 by an American company, HoMedics. Today the brand that started humbly in a cottage in Bilston makes products found in homes all over the world. Here in the UK, the company has a 40 per cent share of the domestic weighing scales market and manufactures the nation's top-selling brand of bathroom scales.

Did you know ... ?

In 1879 some of the Salter workforce formed a football club; having strolled into Wednesbury to buy a football they decided to call themselves West Bromwich Strollers but in 1880 they changed their name to West Bromwich Albion. When the team won the FA Cup in 1888, seven players were Salter employees.

Sellotape – a sticky affair since 1937

An early print advert for Sellotape described it as the 'home handyman number one' because of its ability to repair, secure and seal. In many ways Sellotape still fulfils that function today and while it may not have been the first adhesive cellulose tape to hit the market – that honour falling to 3M's Scotch Tape, introduced in the USA in 1930 – in many parts of the world its name is synonymous with sticky tape.

So what is Sellotape made from? The answer is that it is a biodegradable cellulose film obtained from wood pulp. The pulp itself is sourced from suppliers who engage in extensive reforestation programmes, giving Sellotape first-class green credentials. In fact, the product has been the recipient of a British Office Systems and Stationery Federation environmental award every year since 1996.

The product was developed in 1937 by Colin Kininmonth and George Gray. While little is known about Gray, it seems that Kininmonth came from a scientific background, having obtained a B.Sc. Tech degree at Manchester University in 1907 and worked as a 'technical expert' in Birkdale in 1911. Setting up a firm called Adhesives Tapes, the pair started producing Sellotape and other self-adhesive tapes from premises in Acton, West London and later in Borehamwood, Hertfordshire. At the time of writing the brand belongs to the German Henkel Consumer Adhesives but it is based at Winsford in Cheshire.

Servis Washing Machines – taking the load since 1929

In the dreary days before washing machines, doing the weekly laundry required a strong back and a great deal of energy. Happily, during the first decade of the twentieth century an American called Alva J. Fisher invented an electric-powered machine to do the job and before too long the innovation caught on in the UK.

The firm responsible for the first all-electric British-made washing machine was Wilkins and Mitchell, a power press manufacturer established during the 1890s in Darlaston in the West Midlands by Walter Wilkins and Tom Mitchell. Walter Wilkins made business trips to the USA and it was on one of these that he caught sight of one of the new-fangled washers. On his return home he mentioned it to his wife, an astute lady called Louisa who immediately saw the potential for such a machine in Britain. The result was the Model A, the first Servis washing machine which looked rather like a large metal tub resting on top of a three-legged stool. The 1930s brought the Model E, the first Servis machine to be enclosed in a cabinet, and the Model G which had a pump fitted to dispel the water instead of it having to drain into a bucket.

Following the death of Walter Wilkins in 1946, Servis was run by his widow and then by Henry, his son. In the 1960s, innovations in washing-machine technology saw Servis make their first tumble dryer, shortly followed by their first automatic washing machine. Surviving some tricky times in the Eighties, in 1991 the business was acquired by Antonio Merloni SpA, an Italian white goods company which encountered difficulties of its own in 2008. As a result the Servis brand was bought in 2011 by Vestel, a Turkish-based manufacturer of consumer electronics and home appliances.

Singer Sewing Machine – synonymous with sewing since 1851

Isaac Merritt Singer, the man behind the world's most famous sewing machine brand, was a colourful character noted almost as much for his rackety lifestyle as for his exceptional business achievements. The eighth child of impoverished German immigrants, he was born in Schaghiticoke, New York, but left home at the age of twelve. For many years he had an eclectic career, working when he could as an actor and filling in at other times with manual jobs. A dedicated ladies' man, he became entangled with a succession of women, some of whom he married. Along the way he fathered at least twenty-four children, not always in wedlock.

During a spell in Boston in 1850 he lodged with a man who sold and repaired a type of sewing machine that had an unfortunate tendency to break down. After studying one of these machines, Singer decided that he could improve on its design. Eleven days later he had come up with the world's first practical sewing machine, a design boasting many innovative features including a transverse shuttle and a treadle to generate power. He patented his design in 1851 and, with the backing of a lawyer called Edward Clark, formed I.M. Singer & Company. Using his innate showmanship to promote his invention, Singer managed to become the USA's leading sewing-machine manufacturer within two years.

In 1855 the opening of an office in Paris marked Singer's overseas expansion, an exercise that proved so successful that by 1861 foreign sales were higher than those at home. By now enormously wealthy, Singer fled to Europe in the 1860s to escape his increasingly complicated domestic arrangements. In Paris he met and subsequently married another woman, the beautiful Isabelle Boyer who bore him yet more children. In 1871 he relocated to England, making his new home in Devon where he died in 1875. He is buried in Torquay Cemetery.

The company founded by Isaac Singer continues to innovate and hold its own in an increasingly competitive marketplace. It is now part of SVP Worldwide.

Did you know ... ?

One of Singer's wives, Isabella Boyer, is believed to have been the model for the Statue of Liberty which was designed and executed by her lover, Frédéric-Auguste Bartholdi.

Tupperware – keeping things fresh since 1946

If you've ever popped some food leftovers into a plastic container, you owe a debt of thanks to Earl Tupper, the American inventor and businessman who gave the world Tupperware. Born in New Hampshire in 1907, Tupper learned to turn his hand to just about anything on his family's small farm. After leaving school he took a number of jobs before establishing his own tree surgery business. It was following the failure of this venture in 1936 that Tupper gained experience in the plastics industry by

taking a job with DuPont. Although he stayed with them just one year, he learned enough to set up a company specialising in industrial plastics, often working as a subcontractor for DuPont. After a few years he turned his attention to the consumer market. Having developed a formula for turning black polyethylene slag – a by-product of the petroleum industry – into a mouldable, flexible and durable plastic, he then created an airtight and watertight lid for the containers made from his plastic.

Expecting to amaze American housewives with his invention, Tupper instead hit a wall of indifference. The concept of Tupperware was so avant-garde that it needed to be explained but staff at busy department stores couldn't spare the time to demonstrate and as a result, the new product failed to shift. Undeterred, Tupper made contact with Brownie Wise, a saleswoman of remarkable ability who pioneered the idea of home party plans. With her help, Tupperware Home Parties was born.

Selling his company in 1958, Earl Tupper moved to an island in Central America. He died in Costa Rica in 1983. Brownie Wise, who died in 1992, is about to become the subject of a biopic starring Sandra Bullock. Today Tupperware Brands Inc. is based in Florida.

Velcro – miraculous fastening since 1952

Velcro is one of the overlooked heroes of modern society; millions of us use it every day without ever stopping to wonder how it works or who invented it. To take the latter point first, the genius behind Velcro was a Swiss electrical engineer called Georges de Mestral. He was out with his dog one day when he observed that the animal was covered in burdock burrs which had latched on to its hair and took some effort to shift. Intrigued by the clingy properties of the burrs, Mestral examined them under a microscope where he observed that they were covered in tiny hooks that attached themselves to passing fur or fabric.

The observation prompted Mestral to develop a two-part fabric fastener with myriads of burr-inspired hooks on one part and an equal number of loops on the other; when pressed together, the hooks latched on to the loops, forming a bond firm enough to hold but easy enough to pull apart when required. By combining *velours* and *crochet*, the French words for velvet and hook, he came up with the name Velcro for his invention. Although Mestral completed his first version in 1948, he didn't patent

Did you know...?

Fixed inside every astronaut's helmet is a small piece of Velcro, put there to help with itchy noses.

it until 1952; even then there was a delay of several years during which he tweaked various elements before Velcro was introduced to a grateful public.

Georges de Mestral died in Switzerland in 1990. Today the Velcro brand belongs to Velcro Industries, a privately held, Curacao-based global concern involved in many different markets including consumer, medical, military and construction.

Gone but not forgotten: Brother Typewriters

Brother Industries was founded in Japan in 1908 but the company had a strong UK connection thanks to its factory at Wrexham in Wales where around six million electronic typewriters were produced between 1985 and 2012. When the last typewriter rolled off the production line in 2012 it was given to the Science Museum.

Honourable mention: Dyson Vacuum Cleaners

Frustrated by the poor performance of his vacuum cleaner, James Dyson invented cyclonic vacuuming in 1983. Today Dyson is a brand admired all over the world and the innovations keep coming.

Chapter 7

Health, Hygiene and Household Cleaning

A ccording to the ancient Hebrew proverb, cleanliness is next to godliness. Methodist founder John Wesley agreed, stating in a sermon of 1769 that 'cleanliness is indeed next to godliness'. Modern medicine concurs; thanks to the pioneering work of doctors and scientists in the nineteenth century, we now know that good hygiene practices can prevent the spread of contagious diseases. All of which explains why our shops are fairly brimming with branded products specifically created to keep us, our homes and everything within them as clean, fragrant and healthy as possible. Of course, waging war on germs won't protect us from cutting a finger or getting a headache but happily the manufacturers have a solution for all those problems, too, and many more besides.

While some believe that we should be reducing our reliance on modern cleaning materials and returning to the old-fashioned methods employed by our grandparents – using newspaper and vinegar to clean windows, for example – there's no doubt that ready-to-use branded products offer a more convenient solution when time is of the essence. The same argument applies to over-the-counter health remedies; there has been a resurgence of interest in herbal medicines but when faced with a pounding headache and an important deadline, who wouldn't prefer to swallow a couple of tablets with a proven track record than spend precious minutes preparing a herbal concoction that may or may not relieve the pain?

The reality is that since we all lead such busy lives today, proprietary branded products are likely to be in demand for the foreseeable future. Indeed, those featured in this chapter have been trusted by the British public for at least half a century, many of them for considerably longer. That's not to say they are better than any natural alternatives, just that we would have difficulty in adapting to life without them.

Anadin – banishing headaches since 1932

Anadin made its debut on the UK market in 1932 although as Anacin it has been relieving pain in America since 1918. Formulated by an American dentist called William Milton Knight, the analgesic was brought to Britain by Wyeth, the pharmaceuticals titan.

The only brand in the UK adult pain relief category to offer a product range which includes ibuprofen, paracetamol and aspirin, Anadin's position as a pain-relief brand leader was achieved by a series of clever advertisements including the memorable: 'Tense nervous headache? Nothing works faster than Anadin.' This apparently simple slogan proved extremely effective and was used for thirty years. More recently, the product was presented as the solution for busy people who don't have the time to feel unwell with the strapline: 'For people who just get on with it'.

Today there are several Anadin varieties including Anadin Extra, Anadin Ultra and Anadin Joint Pain. Since 2009 the brand has been owned by Pfizer, one of the world's largest consumer healthcare companies.

HEADACHE?
Nothing acts faster than **ANADIN**

'Anadin' tablets are available from chemists and stores everywhere

Did you know ... ?

In 1995 *New Tricks* actress Tamzin Outhwaite appeared as a teacher in an Anadin TV commercial.

Andrex – soft and strong since 1942

Amazingly, the first purpose-designed lavatory paper was not produced commercially until the mid-nineteenth century. Prior to that, people used whatever was available; in Ancient Rome, a stick with a sponge affixed to one end proved popular, while other cultures favoured scraps of fur, leaves, wads of grass and even corncobs. During the fourteenth century the Chinese developed the world's first bespoke loo paper but since its use was restricted to members of the Imperial Family, the rest of humanity carried on as before. It was only when printed matter – newspapers, catalogues, journals and so on – became readily available to the masses that paper became the material of choice for lavatory hygiene. Even then, it was another hundred years or so before an American called Joseph Gayetty saw that there was a market for paper designed specifically for the lavatory. At first it came in single sheets but within a decade or so paper in continuous rolls had become available.

By 1880 lavatory paper was being produced in Britain although, as was the case in other countries, the paper was hard and not at all absorbent, rather like greaseproof paper, in fact. That only changed in 1942 when the St Andrews Paper Mill in Walthamstow created a soft, two-ply lavatory paper. Initially called Androll, after some modifications the new product was renamed Andrex, a paper so soft it was like using cotton wool, according to the adverts. The nation concurred and Andrex soon became a household favourite.

After several changes of ownership, Andrex is now part of Kimberly-Clark Worldwide and the paper is manufactured in Barrow rather than Walthamstow. Happily, however, real Labrador puppies, introduced as the Andrex mascots in 1972, have returned to adverts following their replacement in 2010 by CGI alternatives.

Did you know ... ?

According to the Andrex website, one in ten UK homes has an Andrex puppy toy.

Brasso – a shining example since 1905

Owned today by the Reckitt Benckiser Group, the UK's best-known metal polish originated in Hull although its ancestry lies in the more exotic climes of Australia.

In the mid-nineteenth century, the fledgling Hull firm that came to be known as Reckitt and Sons established itself as a significant player in the manufacture of four key household necessities: starch, laundry blue, metal polish and washing paste. Employing more than fifty people, by 1854 the company was producing twenty-two distinct products within the basic four categories.

In order to facilitate further expansion, in 1864 the Reckitts started exporting their products to Canada, followed in 1886 by the opening of the firm's first overseas branch in Australia. Some eighteen years later a senior employee discovered an effective liquid metal polish whilst visiting the Australian office. A sample taken back to Hull was analysed and then one year later, in 1905, the company launched a liquid metal polish called Brasso. Initially targeted at railways, hospitals and hotels, it soon became popular with a wider public who found it preferable to the somewhat messier paste polishes.

Brillo – super scouring since 1913

Invented in Brooklyn, New York in 1913 by a cookware salesman and his brother-in-law who happened to be a jeweller, Brillo pads initially came with two components: a wad of fine steel wool for scouring the dirty pots and a bar of soap to provide the necessary lather. With financial help from an attorney called Milton Loeb, the brothers-in-law patented their invention as Brillo, an obvious play on 'brilliant', and went into production.

By 1921 demand for the pads was so high that a new production plant was opened in London, Ohio. However, the most decisive move in the brand's history came in the 1930s when the pads were pre-filled with soap, thereby removing the need for two separate components. At the time of writing, the Brillo brand is owned in the UK by S.C. Johnson and in the USA by Armaly Brands.

Did you know ... ?

In 1964 Andy Warhol stunned the art world by creating *Brillo Boxes*, a series of plywood sculptures replicating the Brillo pad packaging.

Cussons Imperial Leather – luxury bathing since 1938

If you think about it, Imperial Leather isn't the most obvious name for a luxury soap brand but that hasn't prevented it from becoming indelibly associated with a spot of pampering. Comedian Peter Kay remembers a bar of Imperial Leather appearing every Christmas Eve as it was deemed too special for anything but high days and holidays. It's a sentiment that would have pleased Count Orlof, an eighteenth-century Russian aristocrat  who asked perfume experts Bayleys of Bond Street to create a fragrance reminiscent of the imperial Russian court. The resulting scent, Eau de Cologne Imperial Russe, was inspired by the quality Russian leatherwork much favoured by those in imperial circles.

The story then fast-forwards to the early decades of the twentieth century when Bayleys of Bond Street was acquired by Alexander Tom Cussons of the Cussons soap company. In the 1930s, Cussons hit on the idea of using Eau de Cologne Imperial Russe to fragrance a brand-new toilet soap. In its first incarnation it was called Imperial Russian Leather but in 1938 this was simplified to Imperial Leather. During the Second World War when soap was rationed, Cussons' promoted Imperial Leather with the claim that it lasted longer than other brands.

In 1976 Cussons was acquired by PZ, a global healthcare manufacturer established in 1879. The company is now known as PZ Cussons.

Did you know … ?

When soap manufacturers began advertising on television in the Fifties, the programmes they sponsored became known as 'soaps'.

Domestos – germ warfare since 1929

One of Britain's best known household cleaning products, Domestos was produced by an industrial chemist called William Handley in Byker, Newcastle, in 1929. Containing sodium hypochlorite, which is the source of chlorine in swimming pools, in those early days Domestos was sold to housewives by salesmen travelling door-to-door on bicycles. They dispensed it into stoneware jars, ready to be diluted when needed – usually for whitening cotton and household surfaces.

In the 1950s the Domestos brand became involved in campaigns to encourage polio vaccinations. At the end of the same decade, the famous catchphrase 'Domestos kills all known germs' was introduced. Acquired by Lever Bros in 1961, it is now part of Unilever and is available in thirty-five countries, in some of which it goes by a different name.

Elastoplast – speedy healing since 1929

Nowadays, when we suffer a superficial cut we clean the wound and then apply a sticking plaster; job done. But prior to the invention of Elastoplast in 1929, that was not an option. (In America a similar product called Band-Aid had just become available but it was not exported for several decades.) Back then, there was no option but to apply a bandage to the cleaned wound. This was far from ideal because a cumbersome bandage could prevent people with fairly minor injuries from getting on with their lives. (One just has to imagine contestants in *The Great British Bake Off* struggling to complete their baking challenges with their fingers heavily bandaged to appreciate the inconvenience of the situation.)

Fortunately, T. J. Smith and Nephew of Hull were aware of the problem and had come up with a solution by the end of the 1920s. Originally a firm of dispensing chemists, Smith and Nephew had by this time moved into the medical supplies business. In 1929 they announced in the *British Medical Journal* a breakthrough adhesive bandage which they called Elastoplast. At first the new product was intended specifically for doctors but before long consumers were able to purchase their own supplies from pharmacies. A waterproof version of Elastoplast was launched in 1946. The brand is owned today by Beiersdorf AG.

Fairy Liquid – keeping hands soft since 1960

Launched in 1960 by Thomas Hedley & Co, the established British soap manufacturer which had been acquired by US giant Proctor & Gamble in 1930, Fairy Liquid quickly became the UK's leading name in washing-up liquid. In fact, for a household brand that has been with us for less than sixty years, Fairy Liquid's impact has been nothing less than extraordinary, with many using 'Fairy' as a synonym for dish detergent. This success can be attributed to a number of different things, amongst them the brand's claim that it lasts longer than cheaper alternatives. Then there's the original, iconic white bottle complete with an image of a nappy-wearing baby; how many of us pounced on those bottles the moment they were empty in order to transform them into a Blue Peter-style project?

However, there can be no doubt that it was a series of iconic TV ads that played the most significant role in the Fairy Liquid success story. First came the cute mother-

Did you know ... ?

Fairy Liquid ads in the early Seventies featured a very young Patsy Kensit, later to achieve success as an adult in films such as *Lethal Weapon 2* and *Absolute Beginners*.

and-daughter ads in black and white, where women with cut-glass accents told their little girls that Fairy Liquid was kind to their hands, followed by a beautifully-sung jingle explaining that 'hands that do dishes can feel as soft as your face'. By the Eighties actress Nanette Newman was telling consumers that as well as being soft and mild, Fairy could wash 50 per cent more dishes than other brands. These commercials proved so popular that the actress returned in 2010 for a special advert to celebrate Fairy Liquid's 50th anniversary. More recently, in 2002 TV chef Ainsley Harriott was signed by Proctor & Gamble to star in a series of Fairy Liquid commercials.

Germolene – soothing minor injuries since 1922

Childhood grazes and insect bites always felt much better after an application of Germolene, the distinctively-scented pink ointment which came in a small, round tin. Nowadays, the pink ointment and tin are no more, having been replaced by a white cream which is squeezed from a blue tube. However, the old familiar pink lives on as part of the brand's modern packaging livery.

Germolene was introduced early in the 1920s by the Veno Drug Company. Its founder, a Scotsman called William Veno, was actually born William Varney but he changed his name by deed poll to Veno after patenting his famous Veno's cough syrup. Knighted in 1920, he sold his company to the growing Beechams empire five years later and subsequently became involved in a number of unsuccessful business ventures. Facing mounting debts, he took his own life in 1933.

Following a number of mergers and acquisitions, the Germolene brand is now owned by the Bayer company.

Gillette Safety Razors – safer shaving since 1904

Before the invention of the safety razor, shaving was a somewhat perilous business. Men keen to remain smooth of cheek had two options: they could use the services of a professional barber or learn to wield a cut-throat razor themselves. Both options had their downsides. The first could prove costly, especially for those requiring a daily shave, while the second carried the risk of painful nicks or worse.

Did you know … ?

Vintage Gillette razors are widely collected by shaving enthusiasts; sought-after models such as the Fatboy can sell for over £100.

To solve the shaving problem, during the latter years of the nineteenth century a number of inventors attempted to devise a razor that could be relied on to deliver a smooth shave without inflicting injury. Most notable amongst these early inventions was the Star Safety Razor, patented in the USA by Frederick and Otto Kampfe around 1880. Although it featured a skin guard to prevent cuts, the Kampfe brothers' design had a drawback in that its blade needed to be removed frequently for sharpening. The real breakthrough came in 1895 when King Camp Gillette, a travelling salesman from Wisconsin, dreamed up the idea of a safety razor with disposable blades.

Having conceived the idea, Gillette was faced with the task of making his invention a reality. After several years of trial and error, his safety razor and disposable blades went into production in Boston, Massachusetts under the auspices of the Gillette Safety Razor Company. The enterprise was given a considerable boost when the US military equipped their troops with Gillette safety razors during the First World War.

Still based in Boston, today Gillette is owned by Proctor & Gamble.

Macleans Toothpaste – keeping teeth white since 1927

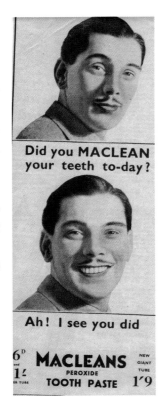

'Did you Maclean your teeth today?' That was the strapline from a series of high-profile advertisements promoting the toothpaste during the 1950s. At that point the brand was owned by the Beechams group which had acquired it from its creator, New Zealand-born Alex C. Maclean, in 1938. Maclean started making health-related products in 1919 but it wasn't until 1927 that he launched his Macleans Peroxide Toothpaste, the world's first proprietary whitening toothpaste.

Following a series of high-level mergers, the Macleans brand is now owned by GlaxoSmithKline.

Persil – a laundry legend since 1909

A century or so ago, doing the laundry was something of a chore. Without washing machines, the weekly wash was both time-consuming and arduous. In Britain, most women (because in those days the task was invariably performed by women) made Monday their wash-day. Rising early, they would heat the water before getting on with hours of pounding, scrubbing and rinsing, all the while praying for the right weather to enable them to get the wash dry.

In the early years of the twentieth century their task was made easier by the ingenuity of two German men, Professor Herman Giessler and Dr Herman Bauer. The name they chose for their invention, the world's first soap powder with a bleaching agent, was Persil, formed from two of the powder's constituents, sodium perborate and silicate. Arriving in the UK in 1909, it was hailed as the 'Amazing Oxygen Washer' because, according to advertisements, its suds were charged with living oxygen. During the 1920s the brand was promoted to housewives via demonstrations performed in a 33ft touring caravan. The following decade, Persil experts visited millions of households in order to demonstrate how the washing powder could help with their laundry.

Currently the UK's leading premium brand laundry detergent, Persil is available in a number of different formats including capsules and liquids. Available in twenty-three countries worldwide, the brand is owned by Henkel AG but is licensed in the UK by Unilever.

Did you know ... ?

Persil is the French word for parsley.

Radox – soothing our aches since 1908

Bath products are big business in the UK. A recent study estimated that our bathing market is worth around £665 million, with bath additives accounting for £150 million of the total – and we buy more bottles of Radox than any other bath additive. That's quite impressive for a brand that started out as a product for reviving tired feet.

Created in 1908 by E. Griffiths Hughes of Manchester, Radox acquired its name by combining the first three letters of the word 'radiated' with the first two of 'oxygen'. Feet continued to be the brand's focus throughout the Twenties but gradually it expanded to encompass a whole body bathing experience. Radox Salts began to be added to baths across the country and from the Fifties onwards, consumers became familiar with the slogan 'Relax in a Radox Bath'.

The first major product diversification came in 1969 when Radox bath liquid was launched, offering a 'secret blend of thirteen soothing herbs and minerals'. Then, as showering grew in popularity, the first Radox shower product was launched in 1975, complete with a convenient hanging hook. In more recent times, innovations involving essential oils, aromatherapy and fragrances have ensured that one in four baths taken in the UK feature a Radox product.

Ownership of the Radox brand has changed several times over the years. E. Griffiths Hughes was acquired by Aspro-Nicholas in 1960, which in turn was taken over in 1984 by the Sara Lee Corporation who sold the brand to Unilever in 2009.

Surf – whitening the wash since 1959

Reportedly the UK's favourite value brand laundry detergent, Surf first appeared on the market in 1959. Its roots, however, can be traced back some seventy-five years to the launch of a product called Sunlight Soap.

In 1884 William Hesketh Lever and his brother James founded a soap company called Lever & Co, the name changing in 1890 to Lever Brothers Ltd. The firm's first product was Sunlight, a household soap with good lathering qualities thanks to the inclusion of pine kernel oil. Unlike other soaps of the time which had to be cut from large blocks, Sunlight was sold in smaller pre-wrapped bars. A philanthropist as well as an entrepreneur, Lever's mission was to make good hygiene accessible to all, to reduce women's workload and to generally enable his customers to enjoy a better quality of life.

By the end of 1887, with his company producing 450 tons of Sunlight soap every week, Lever purchased land on the Wirral shore of the Mersey. Here he built Port Sunlight, a much larger factory together with a modern, purpose-built village for his employees. In 1899 Sunlight Flakes became available, the name changing to Lux Flakes one year later. The advantage of the pre-flaked soap was that it was more convenient to use for laundry purposes than the hard bars of Sunlight. The first step towards modern laundry detergents such as Surf had just been taken.

Did you know ... ?

Birds of a Feather actresses Linda Robson and Pauline Quirke starred in a series of Surf television commercials in the 1990s; in 2014, Ms. Robson described the adverts as the most lucrative job of her career.

When Lever Brothers merged with a Dutch margarine company in 1930, the organisation's name changed to Unilever. By this time the business had expanded all over the world and had spread into different markets including food production. Soap remained a cornerstone of the company, however, and when a detergent brand called Rinso was found to be failing, it was discontinued and replaced with a new product called Surf.

Vaseline – first aid in a jar since 1872

It was recently estimated that a jar of Vaseline is sold every thirty-nine seconds somewhere in the world. That's pretty good going for a product whose origins lie in a sticky substance found on the drill rods of a Pennsylvania oil rig.

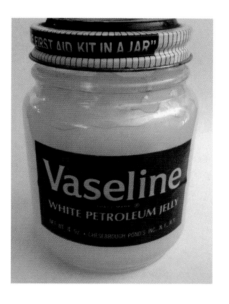

The rise from gloopy petroleum by-product to global bathroom cabinet staple came about thanks to the observational powers of Robert Chesebrough, a young, British-born chemist making a way for himself in nineteenth century America. Whilst visiting a Pennsylvania oil town on a fact-finding mission, 22-year-old Chesebrough noticed the rig workers' habit of slathering the matter they called rod wax onto their skin burns and other injuries in order to speed up the healing process.

Intrigued, Chesebrough set to work experimenting with the substance. It took a fair amount of trial and error but in 1865 he was able to patent a process for making a clear, pure product which he dubbed petroleum jelly. By 1870 he had opened a factory in Brooklyn but when the public didn't immediately recognise the benefits of his 'Wonder Jelly', he resorted to extreme measures to get his message across. Travelling by horse and cart, he demonstrated the product to communities throughout New York State, applying his miracle product to self-inflicted burns whilst at the same time showing his audiences earlier injuries that had already healed. Believing that a new name might also help, in 1872 Chesebrough registered his petroleum jelly as Vaseline, a name arrived at by combining *wasser* – the German word for water – with *élaion*, the Greek word for oil. The dual strategies worked because in 1874, 1,400 jars of Vaseline were being sold daily across the USA. Once Vaseline had caught on, customers must have wondered how they ever lived without it. One of its most common uses was as a preventative for nappy rash but it also became an essential commodity for anyone exposed to very cold temperatures. Its properties in this regard were put to good use when Commander Robert Peary used the product to protect his skin when he made his attempt on the North Pole in 1909.

Robert Chesebrough was knighted by Queen Victoria in 1883; he died in 1933 at the age of 96. As for his company, in 1955 it merged with Pond's to form Chesebrough-Ponds, Inc which in turn was acquired by Unilever in 1987.

Did you know ... ?

There is a type of vintage glass commonly known to collectors as Vaseline glass; the glass is pale yellow with an oily sheen, hence the name, but it turns bright green under ultraviolet light thanks to its uranium oxide content.

Wisdom/Addis – looking after our teeth since 1780

Though few of us know it, we owe a lot to one William Addis, inventor of the toothbrush. According to some accounts, Addis was a colourful character who came up with the idea for a tooth cleaning device whilst serving thirty days in Newgate gaol for his part in a drunken brawl. Whether or not that particular story is true, there is no doubt that in 1780 Addis established a company in Whitechapel after developing a prototype toothbrush from bone and horsehair. By 1796 business was good enough for Addis to need larger premises. When Addis died in 1808 his son took over and continued to grow the business, resulting in a further move in 1840, this time to Hoxton.

During the 1860s the Addis company began automating its manufacturing process, one of the first UK businesses to do so. Overseas expansion soon followed, with exports to the USA starting in the 1880s and spreading to the British Empire and beyond by 1913. At this point not everyone brushed their teeth on a daily basis but after Addis toothbrushes were supplied to the troops during the First World War, the habit became much more widespread.

The 1920s saw further expansion for Addis. When Boots began selling Addis toothbrushes priced at 1 shilling, production began at a new factory in Hertford in order to keep up with demand. By the start of the Second World War, Addis were employing around 650 people. One year later, the first nylon toothbrush was produced under the Wisdom brand name, and bone handles were phased out in 1947. After the war, Addis branched out into kitchen plastics and brushware with the company running its first TV commercial in 1959.

The Addis family continued to own Wisdom Toothbrushes until 1996 when they sold to a management buy-out. At the time of writing, Wisdom Toothbrushes Ltd is based in Haverhill, Suffolk and is owned by a Norwegian dental manufacturer called Jordan AS.

Did you know ... ?

In 1923 Addis provided the tiny toothbrushes for Queen Mary's famous dolls' house; today the house is on permanent display at Windsor Castle.

Gone but not forgotten: Bronco

Remembered for looking like tracing paper and feeling rather scratchy and uncomfortable, Bronco lavatory paper was manufactured in Hackney Wick by the British Patent Perforated Paper Company. Having lost significant ground to softer papers, it was discontinued in 1989.

Chapter 8

The High Street and Beyond

People often grumble about the gradual homogenisation of Britain's high streets, in particular claiming that the prevalence of the nationwide chains makes it hard for smaller shopkeepers to compete. While this may be true, it is worth remembering that many of today's retail empires grew from very humble origins. During the nineteenth century, rapid urban expansion created endless opportunities for those with an entrepreneurial streak. Hard work, resilience and a large dollop of good luck were needed to gain a foothold in the competitive retail market and even then, success was by no means guaranteed. And when it was achieved, the shop founders often died before they were able to enjoy the fruits of their success, leaving their children to continue their work and take their enterprises on to the next level. Nevertheless, these high-street pioneers didn't just change the fortunes of their own families, they also altered our shopping habits.

Boots the Chemist – dispensing good health since 1849

As a massively successful retail brand, Boots exemplifies the idea that 'mighty oaks from little acorns grow'. At the time of writing, there are approximately 2,500 branches of Boots in the UK, meaning that 90 per cent of the population is within a ten-minute drive of one of their shops. While there's no way to be certain, it's a fair bet that founder John Boot never dreamed of achieving such market dominance when he opened his small herbal remedies business in Nottingham in 1849. Boot started his adult life as an agricultural labourer but with help from his father-in-law and chapel community he scraped together enough money to open a shop at 6, Goose Green. There he and his wife Mary sold their home-prepared remedies to customers unable to afford the services of a qualified doctor. Yet Boot was unable to heal himself, succumbing to illness in 1860; after his death, Mary ran the business with Jesse, her ten-year-old son, helping wherever possible.

When Jesse came of age he became a partner in the business and by 1877 he had assumed full control. Now things began to change. One of his most important decisions was to start selling proprietary brands, buying them in bulk to obtain good discounts and then selling on at prices the working classes could afford. When this policy resulted in increased revenue, he was able to move into larger premises and start opening a string of shops throughout the city. In 1884 two new milestones were reached: the first shops outside Nottingham were opened (in Lincoln and Sheffield) and a qualified pharmacist was employed to work within a Boots store. This was just the beginning because by 1914 there were 550 Boots shops nationwide, selling everything from pharmaceutical products and cosmetics to stationery and fancy goods.

Following a series of complicated mergers, Boots is owned today by Walgreen Boots Alliance.

Did you know ... ?

For many years you could have your pictures framed at Boots and, at larger branches, borrow a library book and enjoy a cup of tea in the in-store café. Although the cafés are long gone and the last library closed in 1966, Boots remains a trusted, permanent fixture on our high streets.

Debenhams – much in store since 1813

The Debenhams story began in 1778 when one Thomas Clark set up shop in London's Wigmore Street, selling fancy fabrics and associated fripperies such as bonnets, gloves and parasols. When nineteen-year-old William Debenham arrived on the scene in 1813, he paved the way for modest expansion. New premises bearing the name Debenham & Clark were opened across the street, while the existing shop became Clark & Debenham. Five years later a new branch was opened in the fashionable spa town of Cheltenham and further stores followed in due course.

The business prospered and diversified throughout the nineteenth century, adding a wholesale element to the existing retail stores. In 1851 Thomas Clark retired and his place was taken by William Debenham's brother-in-law, Clement Freebody, whereupon the business became known as Debenham & Freebody. Mergers and acquisitions followed, including the takeover in 1919 of Marshall & Snellgrove and the purchase one year later of Harvey Nichols. In 1927 the Debenhams family ended their long association with the company that bears their name.

Currently owned by Baroness Retail Ltd, Debenhams is now a leading international department store with 240 branches operating in twenty-eight different countries.

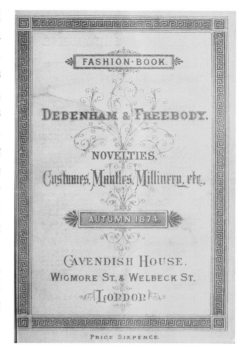

Dorothy Perkins – the height of fashion since 1939

Fondly known to many as 'Dotty P', high-street fashion chain Dorothy Perkins was founded in 1909 by H. P. Newman, although back then it was known as Ladies Hosiery and Underwear Limited. This unexciting name was rendered misleading in 1919 when the shop's twelve branches started offering knitwear and blouses priced at an affordable five shillings alongside their stockings and corsets.

The issue was addressed in 1939 when the wife of a company director suggested changing the name to Dorothy Perkins, a variety of rose given to rambling. By now there were seventy-five shops spread across the country so, whether intentional or not, the rambling analogy was apposite. In 1966 the 250th branch of Dorothy Perkins was opened but it was another eleven years before the brand arrived in London's Oxford Street, then as now one of the busiest and most famous shopping streets in the world.

In 1979 Dorothy Perkins was bought by the Burton Group which became part of the Arcadia Group in 1998. Today, the 600-plus worldwide shops offer a wide variety of women's clothes including 'Petite' and 'Tall' ranges, jeans and maternity wear. It's a far cry from the early days of knickers and stockings.

HMV – music to our ears since 1921

Although this leading technology-based entertainment retailer has had a bumpy ride in recent years, the fact that it seems to have turned the corner under new ownership is good news for the high street as well as for those that prefer browsing for their music, films and games in person as opposed to online.

The origins of the HMV brand lie in the Gramophone Company which used a painting entitled *His Master's Voice* by Francis Barraud to advertise their products. In the original painting a terrier called Nipper listens intently to the sound emanating from the cylinder of a phonograph but the Gramophone Company substituted a wind-up gramophone to make it suit their purposes.

During the early years of the twentieth century the company sold its discs through various independent retailers but in 1921 it opened its first dedicated shop in London's Oxford Street. Known as HMV – an acronym for His Master's Voice – the shop was opened by no less a dignitary that Sir Edward Elgar. While the manufacturing wing of HMV ventured into new areas such as radio and television, the retail operation remained static for several decades. It wasn't until the pop music boom of the Sixties that further shops were opened throughout the London region, spreading out across the country during the Seventies. It was in the Eighties, however, that HMV became a leading national retailer, thanks in no small part to the arrival on the music scene of the CD.

A decade later the advent of the DVD had a similar effect; in 1997 there were 100 HMV shops nationwide but following the introduction of DVDs, by 2004 the number had more than doubled. This growth surge came to an abrupt halt when online shopping began to hit sales. Despite various attempts to reverse the trend, HMV Group plc went into administration in 2013, reappearing under new ownership within a couple of months. Today HMV Retail Ltd has around 120 shops within the UK, a further 110 in Canada and in excess of forty across Ireland.

Harrods – supplying the affluent since 1849

When the Qatari royal family bought the world-famous Knightsbridge department store from Mohammed Al Fayed in 2010, the asking price was an eye-watering £1.5bn. The one-room grocery business founded in the middle of the nineteenth century by Charles Henry Harrod has certainly come a long way.

Originally an Essex lad, Harrod first set up shop as a tea dealer in London's Whitechapel district before becoming a tea wholesaler in Eastcheap. In 1849, keen to capitalise on the influx of wealthy residents into Knightsbridge, he opened the aforementioned one-room shop in the Brompton Road. As the business prospered he took on larger premises and gradually added new lines. His son, Charles Digby Harrod, assumed control of the business in the 1860s and soon proved to be a chip off the old block, building on his father's success so that by 1880 Harrods was an elite department store, offering its affluent clientele luxury goods of every kind.

A destructive fire in December 1883 failed to dent the indomitable Harrod spirit. A palatial new store – designed with gaudy aplomb by architect Charles William

Stephens – was promptly put under construction but in the meantime, so as not to miss out on the lucrative Christmas trade, the store relocated into Humphrey's Hall, a nearby exhibition hall which has since been demolished.

When Harrod retired in 1889 the store became a public company, a state which lasted until 1985 when it was bought, together with parent company House of Fraser, by Egyptian businessman Mohammed Al Fayed. The controversial purchase became the subject of a lengthy legal wrangle.

Did you know … ?

Harrods' motto is *Omnia Omnibus Ubique* which translates as 'All things for all people, everywhere'.

F. Hinds – a bling thing since 1856

Although the jewellery chain F. Hinds has officially been trading since 1856, the Hinds family has been associated with the industry since 1825 when Joseph Hinds set up as a clockmaker in Stamford, Lincolnshire. His son, George Henry, served an apprenticeship with a watchmaker before moving to London where, in 1856, he opened a shop in Paddington. Twenty years later he relocated to the Edgware Road when his original premises were knocked down as part of a road-widening scheme.

As the business prospered new branches of the shop were opened across the city. As the twentieth century dawned, control of the company passed to George's son, William Hinds, with his three sons – William, George and Frank – joining the family concern in due course. During the First World War, George and Frank served in the trenches while their brother William stayed behind to look after the business, taking sole responsibility for it following the death of their father in 1915. One year later brother George was killed in action on the first day of the Battle of the Somme.

After the war, William and Frank shared the management of the company until 1924 when they agreed to an amicable split, each brother taking control of six shops. While William diversified into different areas including cycling, theatre and film (see box below), Frank focused on the jewellery business, opening a new shop in Bristol and steering his business through the tricky economic years of the Thirties.

After the Second World War, during which F. Hinds did their bit by producing timing devices for bombs, Frank's sons Eric and Roy joined the family firm, the fifth generation of Hinds to work in the business. Steady expansion continued, so that by 1973 – ten years after Frank's death – there were forty-seven branches of F. Hinds across south and central England. In the 1980s a sixth generation came into the business when Roy's sons David and Andrew and Eric's son Neil started work at F. Hinds. The same decade saw increased expansion together with a redesign of the existing shops. Today there are 114 F. Hinds shop throughout England and Wales, making the business the UK's largest independent jeweller. The fact that it has remained in the hands of the same family for nearly 160 years makes it something of a rarity in British retail.

> **Did you know … ?**
>
> William Hinds (brother of Frank) was co-founder of Hammer Films, famous for their cult horror movies.

John Lewis – magic with merchandise since 1862

In 1856, when George Hinds was busy opening his first jewellery shop in Paddington, a young man of 20 called John Lewis arrived in London from Somerset. He took a job at the Peter Robinson department store in Oxford Circus and six years later laid the foundations for an Oxford Street department store of his own. However, it was his son, John Spedan Lewis, who was destined to turn the family business into the famous John Lewis Partnership.

The shop Lewis opened at 132 Oxford Street in 1862 was initially a small drapery business but it soon grew into something much bigger. Cramming it full of merchandise, the ambitious young man utilised every inch of space to maximise sales potential. His watchwords were said to be value, assortment, service and honesty. The formula worked so well that by the 1880s the premises were rebuilt to accommodate a full-blown department store. In 1884, at the age of 48, Lewis married 30-year-old Eliza Baker, one of the first women to study at Cambridge's Girton College. Within three years the couple had two sons, John Spedan and Oswald, both of whom were to enter the family business in due course.

In December 1905 the decline of a rival business paved the way for expansion. Hearing that the Peter Jones store in Sloane Square was up for sale, Lewis set off to purchase it with twenty £1,000 banknotes in his pocket. However, acquiring the store proved easier than turning its fortunes around. The situation was rescued when John Spedan assumed control of Peter Jones a few years later. By introducing innovations such as the employment of well-educated young women, he engineered a turnaround in profits and created a contented workforce. In contrast, at the Oxford Street store which was still managed by Lewis Senior, staff were so discontented that they went on strike in 1920.

That same year John Spedan introduced a profit-sharing scheme, driven as much by a social conscience as the belief that an incentivised staff would perform better. In 1929, following the death of his father the previous year, he created the John Lewis Partnership which ultimately resulted in all employees having a stake in the business. During the 1930s the business expanded, acquiring department stores beyond the capital as well as the ten Waitrose shops (see entry for Waitrose). In the early hours of 18 September 1940, the Oxford Street store was obliterated by German incendiary devices although fortunately the 200 people sleeping in the store's air-raid shelter survived unscathed. While a new store was built – a process that took twenty years because of steel shortages – trading continued in nearby premises. In 1953, the acquisition of a Lancashire textile mill enabled John Lewis to produce its own fabric ranges.

John Spedan Lewis retired in 1955 and died in 1963. The business he nurtured through six decades is now the UK's largest department store retailer with forty-four shops and a thriving online presence. The 'never knowingly undersold' motto he introduced at Peter Jones in 1925 is still in use today.

Liberty – aesthetic delights since 1875

Without two random twists of fate, it is probable that London's most eclectic and quintessentially English department store would not exist. The first occurred when Buckinghamshire-born Arthur Lasenby Liberty was prevented from attending university; he had been destined to do so but a reversal in his family's finances rendered the idea impossible. Instead, at the age of 16 he was apprenticed to a draper in London's Baker Street.

The second twist occurred three years later when he took a job at Farmers & Rogers' Great Shawl and Cloak Emporium in Regent Street. The year was 1862 and London had just played host to the second International Exhibition of Industry and Art. A particular highlight of the exhibition had been a display of Japanese artefacts and wares previously unseen in Britain. The imported items created such a sensation that when the surplus was put up for auction following the exhibition's closure, Farmers & Rogers bought enough to stock a new Oriental Warehouse which they opened next door to their existing premises. This was where young Liberty began work in 1862, rising to the position of manager in just two years.

He remained there for a decade, learning his craft and developing an abiding interest in Japanese and oriental design. Convinced that he could impart his enthusiasm to a discerning public, he borrowed £2,000 and on 15 May 1875 opened his own store at 218a Regent Street. Liberty's confidence proved well-founded when fashionable customers drawn from artistic and literary circles flocked to buy his exotic, inspiring wares. Such was his success that within eighteen months he was able to repay his loan and expand the store into adjacent premises. Further expansion followed in 1884 when he pulled off the considerable coup of persuading his friend, the noted architect E. W. Godwin, to establish a specialist dress department. Godwin was a leading exponent of the dress reform movement which emphasised the importance of comfort and freedom of movement in women's dress.

Already established as the commercial home of the Aesthetic Movement, the store now formed links with leading designers of the Art Nouveau movement, notably including Archibald Knox who created his Celtic-inspired silver Cymric ware and pewter Tudric ware exclusively for Liberty. Although the products sold at Liberty were stylistically similar to the artisan-made wares of the Arts & Crafts movement, they differed in that Liberty's products were machine made in order to keep costs down. According to Liberty, his store aspired to 'the production of useful and beautiful objects at prices within the reach of all classes'.

In 1890 a Paris branch of the store was opened and in 1894 Liberty became a public company. Arthur Lasenby Liberty was knighted in 1913 and he retired a year later although he remained a majority shareholder until his death in 1917. The store's famous mock-Tudor building, designed by father and son architects Edwin T. and Edwin S. Hall, and constructed from the timbers of HMS *Impregnable* and HMS *Hindustan*, was not completed until after his death. The Liberty family retained a connection with the store for many years although since 2010 it has been owned by a private equity group.

> ### Did you know … ?
>
> In Italy, the Liberty name is so inextricably linked with the Art Nouveau movement that its Italian name is actually *Stile Liberty*.

Lloyds Bank – counting the pennies since 1765

One of the 'big four' high-street banks, Lloyds – in common with much of the banking sector – has had a rocky ride in recent years. Nevertheless, it remains a force to be reckoned with, employing around 46,000 people and offering banking services to some 16 million individuals and small businesses nationwide. That's a far cry from its origins as Birmingham's first bespoke bank back in 1765.

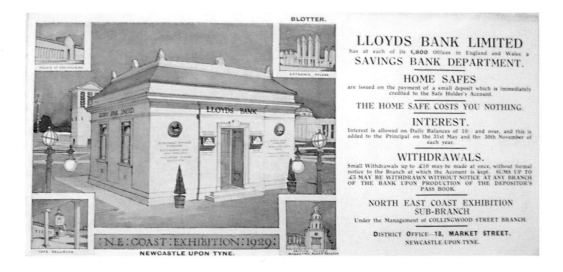

Did you know ... ?

Lloyds' famous black horse symbol was first used in 1677 by Humphrey Stokes, a goldsmith based at London's Lombard Street. By 1728 the horse symbol was being used by John Bland, another Lombard Street goldsmith; over time Bland developed into the firm of Barnetts, Hoares & Co which was acquired by Lloyds in 1884. For a while after this the black horse was used alongside the bank's existing symbol, the beehive, which represented thrift and industry.

When the bank first opened its doors on 3 June 1765, it was known as Taylor and Lloyds. The Taylor in question was John Taylor, Birmingham's famous button king who amassed a fortune manufacturing buttons, small boxes and other 'toy' items. His partner in the banking enterprise was a Birmingham-based Quaker industrialist called Sampson Lloyd. Prior to 1765, both Taylor and Lloyd had lent money to new businesses as a sideline to their main interests. As Birmingham grew in industrial importance, they decided it made sense to join forces and open the city's first official bank.

Taylor died in 1775 with Lloyd following him four years later. Their respective heirs continued to oversee the bank's interests until 1852 when Taylor's descendants bowed out and the bank became known as Lloyds. A few years later, amid a programme of rapid expansion, Lloyds absorbed a number of other banking concerns and relocated its headquarters to London where it remains today.

Marks & Spencer – reliable innovation since 1884

Though we sometimes take it for granted, there's no denying that for most of us, good old M&S is a reliable and comforting presence on our high streets, the retail equivalent, perhaps, of a cosy pair of slippers. Indeed, 33 million of us shop regularly at one of the 852 M&S UK stores (1,330 worldwide) or purchase via their website. Founders Michael Marks and Tom Spencer would surely approve.

The M&S story began in the early 1880s when Jewish immigrant Michael Marks arrived in Leeds, having escaped persecution in what is now Belarus. Speaking little English and without much money to his name, he earned his living as a pedlar but by 1884 was trading from an open stall at Leeds' Kirkgate Market, thanks to a loan from wholesaler Isaac Dewhirst. With the instinctive panache of a born salesman, he attracted customers with the slogan, 'Don't ask the price, it's a penny'.

Prompted, perhaps, by his marriage in 1886 to Hannah Cohen and the subsequent arrival of children, Marks was keen to expand his business. As a result, in September

1894 he went into partnership with Isaac Dewhirst's cashier, Tom Spencer. In the new organisation called Marks & Spencer, Marks provided the sales and merchandising flair while Spencer brought financial and organisational acumen. With such able men guiding it the business flourished so that by 1900 there were thirty-six 'Penny Bazaars' and twelve high-street stores. One year later, a purpose-built warehouse in Derby Street,

Manchester, became the company's headquarters.

In the 1900s Tom Spencer and Michael Marks died within a few years of each other and, after a legal battle, Marks' son Simon took control of the business. Expansion continued; in 1915 there were 145 stores even though the famous penny pricing was abandoned with the advent of the First World War in 1914. In the inter-war years M&S started selling goods priced up to five shillings and began to focus on food and well-made, affordable clothing. When the Second World War began, eating out became popular because rationing wasn't enforced in restaurants and thus people were able to have a good meal without using their precious ration coupons. As a result, by 1942 M&S had opened eighty-two Café Bars in various stores.

After the war, M&S continued to innovate in areas such as clothing and food; frozen food, for example, was introduced in 1972. A year later the company was the first major retailer to start labelling their food products with sell-by dates. Food sales now account for 57 per cent of the company's turnover.

Did you know...?

During the Second World War 100 M&S stores were bombed and sixteen were destroyed completely. Staff did their bit for the war effort by fire-watching, fundraising for a Spitfire and setting up soup kitchens.

Sainsbury's – purveying good food since 1869

When husband and wife team John James and Mary Ann Sainsbury opened a dairy in London's Drury Lane in 1869, they could never have imagined that one day there would be a nationwide chain of 1,200 shops bearing their name, nor that these shops would offer employment to some 161,000 people. At the time, given their modest backgrounds, simply possessing the wherewithal to run a small business of their own must have struck the hardworking couple as no mean achievement.

John Sainsbury was working for an oil and paint merchant near Victoria when he met his future wife, the daughter of Benjamin Staples who owned a small string of dairies. Mary had gained a lot of experience from working in one of her father's dairies so when she and Sainsbury were married in 1869, it made sense for the couple to invest their savings of £100 in a venture selling butter, eggs and milk from a small shop in Drury Lane. While her new husband worked out his notice, Mary took charge of the shop, rising early to ensure the premises were spick and span before darting behind the counter to serve customers with the freshest possible produce.

After four years the Sainsburys had made enough money to open a new dairy in Kentish Town. Leaving trusted employees to run the Drury Lane shop, John and Mary lived above the new premises with their children. In 1875 they opened a second shop in the same street, this one specialising in bacon and ham, and in due course added a third shop. By 1882 they had ventured outside London to Croydon where they opened a rather upmarket branch to cater for the rising middle classes. The Croydon premises were fancier than their London equivalents, with colourful wall tiles, counter fronts decorated with stained-glass pictures of game birds and a marble shop front with gilded lettering. The produce on offer was more elaborate; customers could choose from a variety of cheeses and cooked meats, buy Sainsbury's own-brand pork pies and indulge in an astonishing selection of seasonal poultry and game, all of which could be delivered by errand boys on bicycles, tricycles and, for longer distances, horse and cart.

Expansion continued apace so that by 1922 J. Sainsbury Ltd was the largest grocery concern in Britain. When co-founder John James died six years later – surviving Mary by one year – there were 128 shops. Under the direction of their oldest son, John Benjamin Sainsbury, the business continued to flourish, aided in particular by the acquisition in 1936 of a northern food chain called Thoroughgood. During the Second World War, bomb damage and rationing had a deleterious impact on the business but by 1950 it had bounced back sufficiently for the store's first self-service branch to be opened in Croydon. Gradually, over the ensuing three decades all the traditional counter service stores were replaced by supermarkets.

Successive members of the Sainsbury family played a part in the management of the organisation until David Sainsbury resigned as Chair in 1997. Nevertheless, at the time of writing they still own around 15 per cent of the shares.

Did you know ... ?

To date, three members of the Sainsbury family have received life peerages: Alan Sainsbury (John and Mary's grandson) became Baron Sainsbury of Drury Lane in 1962; his son, John Davan Sainsbury, became Baron Sainsbury of Preston Candover in 1989; and David Sainsbury, great-grandson of the founders, became Baron Sainsbury of Turville in 1997.

W H Smith – in the news since 1792

W. H. SMITH & SON'S RAILWAY BOOKSTALL, VICTORIA STATION, MANCHESTER.

As far as shopping experiences go, there's nothing out of the ordinary about popping into W H Smith to pick up a newspaper and a birthday card. So it might come as a surprise to learn that this Goliath of the modern British high street exists only because of a decidedly extraordinary love match. That was in 1784 when 46-year-old Henry

Walton Smith married 28-year-old Anna Eastaugh. It was not the age disparity that raised eyebrows about the match, however, but class disparity. While Smith came from an affluent Somerset family, while his Suffolk-born bride was a humble servant working for a London coal merchant's widow. Finding his choice of wife socially unacceptable, Smith's family cut off his allowance, forcing him to seek an alternative means of support.

At first he worked for a highly-placed Customs House official where he came into contact with such luminaries of the day as Horace Walpole and Sir Joshua Reynolds. In due course the marriage produced three children: Henry Edward in 1787, Mary Ann in 1790 and William Henry in 1792. This growing family was probably what prompted Smith to leave the excise service and set up with Anna as a news vendor from premises in London's Little Grosvenor Street. Sadly, he died just a few months after embarking on the new venture, leaving Anna to take control of the business (just as Mary Boot was to do following the death of her spouse some sixty-eight years later).

Rising to the challenge, Anna added stationery and other new lines to H W Smith and the shop prospered under her management. Upon her demise in 1816 the business became a partnership run by her sons but this was officially dissolved in 1828, leaving the younger son, William Henry Smith, in sole control. It was at this point that the concern became known as W H Smith. The name was to change again in 1846 when William Henry's own son, confusingly yet another William Henry, was brought into the business on his coming of age. Now known as W H Smith & Son, it began to achieve real success thanks to the rise of the railways.

In the 1840s the railway network expanded across Britain, bringing convenient and relatively cheap transport to almost every town and village. As stations sprang up, William Henry had the vision to realise that passengers would want something to read as they waited for their trains. In consequence, in 1848 he opened a bookstall at Euston Station selling reasonably-priced publications. When this proved a success, he opened more until there were W H Smith & Son bookstalls across the railway network. In order to keep this burgeoning empire supplied, a distribution network was set up with warehouses in Manchester, Birmingham, Liverpool and Dublin, making W H Smith & Son the leading book and newspaper distributor in the country.

In 1857, feeling the time had come to pass the baton on to the next generation, the older William Henry retired to Bournemouth where he built a fine new home which he named Walton House in memory of his father. It was completed in 1861 and he lived there until his death in 1865. Now the younger William Henry was in charge of the family business. One of his first innovations was the introduction of a lending library which lasted just over 100 years. At the same time he developed an interest in politics which led him in 1864 to take on a partner, the barrister William Lethbridge. With Lethbridge running things, Smith was able to pursue his political ambitions, becoming an MP in 1868. Six years later, having stepped back completely from the business, he was appointed First Lord of the Admiralty by Disraeli, despite having no naval experience. He went on to serve as Leader of the House of Commons and First Lord of the Treasury under Salisbury. When he died in 1891, his widow was created Viscountess Hambleden in his honour and on her death in 1913 his son William Frederick became Viscount Hambleden.

Two further generations of Smiths ran the business but their influence gradually lessened when the company went public. The last family member to sit on the board of W H Smith stood down in 1996. Today, after many complicated mergers, demergers and acquisitions, the business is still going strong with 621 high street stores and 740 travel outlets.

Did you know ... ?

W H Smith had a hand in originating the ISBN book-numbering system which today is used worldwide. In 1966 Gordon Foster, Emeritus Professor of Statistics at Trinity College, Dublin, devised a scheme to help the company simplify their book identification by using unique nine-digit sequences called Standard Book Numbering (SBN for short). By 1970 SBN had been adopted as international standard ISO 2108 and a few years later it became known as ISBN (International Standard Book Number).

Waitrose – classy groceries since 1904

In 1904 three ambitious young men – Wallace Waite, Arthur Rose and David Taylor – joined forces to open a high class grocery shop at 263, Acton High Street. At Waite, Rose & Taylor, Waite was responsible for sourcing products and Rose was company secretary and accountant while Taylor managed the shop. From the very first their philosophy was to offer customers a large and varied selection of the finest-quality foodstuffs. Thanks to these principles, despite stiff competition their venture prospered, although perhaps not quickly enough to satisfy Taylor who quit the business in 1906.

In 1908 the shop underwent a change of name; Taylor was removed and Waite and Rose merged to form Waitrose. A merger of a different sort took place two years later when Rose married Waite's sister, Bertha. By now the shop had expanded along the High Street to number 267, with further premises at the rear. They were expanding in other ways, too, taking on more staff and adding hardware, coal and household tools to their stock lines. The next step was to open new branches. Two appeared in 1913 and several more followed in quick succession, most in London although a Windsor shop was opened in 1918.

During the First World War, Rose enlisted while Waite remained at home to hold the fort. After the Armistice, Rose suffered from poor health as a result of wartime injuries and so he left the business in 1924. Now in sole control, Waite continued to open new shops in affluent areas. By 1937 he was thinking about retirement but wanted to make sure his chain of shops was left in safe hands. His solution was to sell the ten Waitrose shops to the John Lewis Partnership on 1 October of that year, staying on to oversee the transition. He retired in 1940, having been awarded an MBE for promoting British and Empire produce, and lived until 1971.

In Waite's time, grocery shopping had been a polite exercise in which the customer waited to be served before handing over a list of required goods to a shop assistant. Things were changing, however, and with the advent of self-service supermarkets in Britain in the 1950s, Waitrose needed to move with the times. Their first supermarket was opened in Streatham in 1955 with 2,500 square feet of selling space. As more followed, a new distribution centre was opened at Bracknell in Berkshire to enable the business to cope with the increased demand. Today Waitrose is a byword in popular culture for aspirational food shopping and there are in excess of 300 Waitrose stores across the country. Not bad going for a little grocery shop from Acton.

Gone but not forgotten: Woolworths

It was only in 2008 that F. W. Woolworths – or Woolies as it was fondly known – disappeared from our high streets so memories remain strong today. The first UK branch of the cut-price American store opened in Liverpool in 1909. When the axe fell just under 100 years later, there were 800 stores across the country, selling everything from children's clothes, toys and sweets to stationery, household goods and CDs and DVDs.

Honourable mention: The Body Shop

Founded by Anita Roddick, the first branch of ethical beauty brand The Body Shop opened in Brighton in 1976. It is now owned by L'Oréal and has 3,000 stores in more than sixty countries.

Chapter 9

The Toy Cupboard

As adults, we often forget things that happened to us yesterday but as a rule childhood memories stay with us through to old age. That might explain why we tend to feel most nostalgic about brands associated with toys and games. The playthings of our younger years take on a rosy glow when we remember them; they were better-made than modern toys, we tell ourselves, and encouraged us to be energetic, imaginative and creative. It may be that our memories are misleading, that it's nothing more than a wistful hankering for our lost days of youth that makes us remember our toys with such fondness. Yet given that many of the brands we knew and loved are as popular today as they were when we were young, it's clear that these classic brands really do possess special qualities. Transcending eras, they bring joy to each successive generation. Long may they last.

Airfix – built for success since 1939

As integral to a traditional British childhood as seaside holidays and rainy Bonfire Nights, the plastic scale model kits made by Airfix have been delighting the UK's youngsters since the Fifties. The man behind the brand was born Miklos Koves, a Hungarian Jew who spent sixteen years moving from one country to another to avoid political and religious persecution. In 1938 he brought his family to London, changed his name to Nicholas Kove and, in 1939, set up a small factory on the Edgware Road, producing cheap air-filled novelties. When choosing the name for his business he opted for one that would appear at the front of business directories, hence 'Air' which also referenced the inflated nature of his products. The 'fix' part, meanwhile, harked back to Interfix, a collar-stiffening product he had previously patented during a sojourn in Italy.

During the Second World War Kove was interned on the Isle of Man but was released once the threat of invasion had passed. After the war he started afresh with his business, acquiring some cutting-edge injection moulding machines in order to manufacture plastic combs. The model kits grew out of a commission Airfix received in 1949 from the Ferguson tractor company who wanted a replica of their latest model

to use as a sales tool. When it proved difficult to create the model in one piece, the decision was taken to break the tractor down into a series of parts which could be manufactured more easily and assembled later. Ferguson gave Airfix permission to produce and sell more tractor models, and this in turn led to a deal with Woolworth's to supply a series of kits. In 1952 a model of Sir Francis Drake's ship *Golden Hind* appeared, followed a year later by the Spitfire which was to become a mainstay of the range.

When Nicholas Kove died in 1958 Airfix was run by former RAF pilot Ralph Ehrmann. Having enjoyed three successful decades, the firm experienced severe financial difficulties in the Eighties. Following bankruptcy, the brand was bought and sold several times; it now belongs to Hornby Hobbies Ltd which also owns Humbrol paints. Thanks to significant investment, a packaging overhaul and the introduction of interesting new models, the situation looks promising for this popular brand.

Did you know ... ?

There was more to Airfix's output than just model kits; in the 1960s, for example, they manufactured Fred, the Homepride flour mascot.

Barbie – career girl and fashion doyenne since 1959

Fashion dolls were available before Barbie appeared on the toy scene but they mostly resembled little girls dressed in grown-ups' clothes, not the stylish young ladies they were meant to represent. One notable exception was Bild Lilli, a doll inspired by a rather racy comic strip character from a German newspaper. Shapely and heavily made-up, Bild Lilli was not marketed as a children's toy but they loved her nevertheless. Nor was her popularity restricted to her homeland; Lilli was exported to several countries including the USA where she may have given Mattel the impetus to launch a fashion doll of their own, complete with trendy hairstyle and a cutting-edge wardrobe.

Barbie's creator was Ruth Handler who, together with her husband Elliot, had founded Mattel Creations in 1945. The official story goes that it was while watching her daughter Barbara invent stories about the lives and careers of her paper dolls that she came up with the idea for a new kind of three-dimensional fashion doll. After a great deal of experimentation, in 1959 Mattel launched Barbie, the Teen-Age Fashion Model at the New York Toy Fair. Sporting a perky ponytail and wearing a black-and-white striped swimsuit, Barbara Millicent Roberts, aka Barbie, was priced at $3 with additional outfits costing from $1 to $5. In her first year, 300,000 Barbie dolls were sold.

Barbie was joined in 1961 by her boyfriend, Ken, who is named after the Handlers' son. In 1963 she acquired a best friend, Midge, followed a year later by a little sister called Skipper. Since then she has acquired two more sisters and several friends, as has Ken whose best friend Alan 'married' Midge in 1991. To date Barbie has experienced more than 150 careers including astronaut, vet, entrepreneur, police officer and nurse. She has run for President six times but has yet to make it to the White House.

Did you know...?

In 2006 a collection of over 4,000 Barbie dolls dating from 1959 to 2002 raised £111,000 when they went under the hammer at Christie's. The sale's star performer, a brunette Barbie from 1965 wearing a very rare 'Midnight Red' evening ensemble, sold for £9,000 including buyer's premium.

Cluedo – murder most fun since 1949

Cluedo was invented by Anthony Pratt, a professional pianist from Birmingham who devised the game during the Second World War as a way of enlivening the blackout. Pratt received encouragement from a neighbour, Geoffrey Bull, who had prior experience in the board games business, having sold Buccaneer, a game of his own invention, to Waddingtons.

With help from his wife Elva who designed the board, Pratt devised a board game loosely inspired by a popular party game called Murder in the Dark. In 1945 the Pratts and the Bulls demonstrated the game to the people at Waddingtons who saw its potential but suggested a few changes such as trimming the characters from ten to six and replacing one of the weapons, a bomb, with a candlestick. Wartime shortages stalled production until 1949 when the game finally went on sale as Cluedo, a combination of 'clue' and the Latin '*ludo*' which translates as 'I play'. Soon afterwards, the game was licensed to Parker Brothers in the USA where it was renamed Clue.

Did you know ... ?

Cluedo (or Clue) is played in more than forty nations worldwide, with the character names varying from country to country. In the USA, for example, murder victim Dr Black becomes Mr Boddy while in Brazil Miss Scarlet is Senorita Rosa and in Switzerland Colonel Mustard changes gender to become Madame Curry.

Sadly for Anthony and Elva Pratt, the game did not set them up for life. Believing that foreign sales were sluggish, in 1953 they assigned their overseas royalties to Waddingtons in exchange for £5,000. This left them with income from British royalties until their patent expired in the 1960s. Attempting to replicate Cluedo's success, Pratt developed two further board games but failed to find a maker for them. Eventually he returned to work, taking a job as a solicitor's clerk. He died in 1994 and is buried in Bromsgrove cemetery. Coincidentally, that same year Waddingtons was bought by Hasbro, the multinational toy and games giant which had acquired Parker Brothers three years previously.

Corgi – toys for the boys since 1956

The first Corgi model vehicles were introduced by Mettoy Ltd in 1956 with a view to rivalling the highly successful Dinky range. Mettoy had been founded in Northampton in 1933 by cousins Philipp Ullmann and Arthur Katz. Both men had worked in the famous Nuremburg toy industry but left Germany once Hitler came to power because they were Jewish. Help with establishing their tinplate toy business came from Simon Marks, son of Marks & Spencer co-founder Michael Marks, an association that continued when M&S became an important customer for Mettoy.

During the Second World War munitions were made at Mettoy's Northampton site and also at a new location in Swansea. After the war, however, toy production resumed, with all manufacturing taking place in Swansea while the focus in Northampton switched to design and development. When the idea for a Dinky-style diecast range was conceived, the factory's Welsh location inspired the directors to name it after the famous Welsh dog breed.

The first Corgi cars to appear in July 1956 were the Ford Consul, Morris Cowley, Austin Cambridge, Hillman Husky, Vauxhall Velox, Rover 90 and Riley Pathfinder. Also in the range were a Bedford 12cwt van and two sports cars, an Austin Healey and a Triumph TR2. The Corgi Model Club was launched that December and the following year the first Corgi catalogue was published. The quality of the products plus some judicious television advertising saw the range achieving sales of nearly 2.75 million pieces by the end of the first trading year. Over the years Corgi produced some memorable vehicles, the most famous of which has to be James Bond's Aston Martin DB5 which won the UK Toy of the Year Award when it debuted in 1965. Priced at 10 shillings and with features no self-respecting 00 Agent could manage without – an ejector seat and front-mounted machine guns – the vehicle was a runaway success with sales approaching the four-million mark within three years.

Having experienced turbulent times including a destructive warehouse fire and financial difficulties, Mettoy ceased trading in 1983 but the Corgi brand survived thanks to a management buyout. Formed in 1984, the Corgi Toy Company was acquired by Mattel in 1989, whereupon production was relocated to Leicester. After further reorganisation and take-overs, Corgi was bought by Hornby, its current owner, in 2008.

Etch A Sketch – drawing with knobs on since 1960

It seems counter-intuitive that children brought up with modern electronic marvels should want to play with an Etch A Sketch, the flat box with a magnetic screen on which simple pictures can be drawn by twisting two knobs, and then erased with a quick shake. Nevertheless, the toy which seemed little short of magical to its first generation of users remains popular today, helped, perhaps, by the fact that it requires no batteries or power connectors to function.

This much-loved plaything was invented by André Cassagnes, a French electrician who observed that the pencil marks he made on the protective cover of an electric light switch appeared on the opposite side, thanks to some metallic particles being drawn through an electrostatic charge. Having adapted the science in order to create a clever new toy which he named Telecran, Cassagnes was unable to patent it due to lack of funds. Undeterred, he found an investor willing to stump up the money but when the patent was filed, a clerical error meant that the person credited with Telecran's invention was Arthur Granjean, the investor's representative who physically filed the patent. Despite the confusion, Cassagnes' legal rights were not affected.

In France the toy remains Telecran to this day but to the rest of the world it became Etch A Sketch when the Ohio Art Company acquired a licence to produce it and then worked with Cassagnes on a modified version. Launched in time for Christmas 1960, the first Etch A Sketch toys were an immediate success with sales for the period exceeding 600,000. In due course new crazes came and went but the Etch A Sketch remained a perennial favourite. Its classic status was given official recognition in 2003 when it was named one of the best toys of the twentieth century by the Toy Industry Association.

Did you know ... ?

An Etch A Sketch character called Etch appears in Pixar's hugely popular *Toy Story* franchise. As one of Andy's toys he plays a supporting role in *Toy Story* and *Toy Story 2* but appears only fleetingly at the start of *Toy Story 3* when it is revealed that he has been re-homed now Andy has grown up.

Fuzzy Felt – making a scene since 1950

Many classic toy brands owe their iconic status to an ingenious or complex design. Not so Fuzzy Felt, which won children's hearts with its very simplicity, since creating scenes by applying colourful felt shapes to a textured background is an activity any child can enjoy, regardless of ability. Small wonder that since Fuzzy Felt made its debut in 1950, an estimated 26.25 million boxes have been sold.

What makes this all the more remarkable is that for its first twenty years, Fuzzy Felt operated as something of a cottage industry. It was started by Lois Allan, née Day, an American who studied art and dress design in Paris before marrying Peter Allan, an Englishman. Before the Second World War the couple ran a travel agency in Buckinghamshire but when her husband joined the RAF, Mrs Allan decided to make her own contribution to the war effort by creating felt gaskets for use in tanks. Working from outbuildings at her home in Farnham Common, she was helped by local women who brought their offspring to a crèche set up by Mrs Allan. It was watching these children play with some felt off-cuts that gave Mrs Allan the inspiration for Fuzzy Felt. After the war she spent a few years turning her idea into a viable product before presenting it to the toy buyers at John Lewis and Heals. They liked what they saw and so, in 1950, Fuzzy Felt was born.

By 1972 the Fuzzy Felt operation, now trading as Allan Industries Ltd, was too big for the Farnham Common outbuildings so it relocated to new premises in High Wycombe where it remained for many years. Since 2009 Fuzzy Felt has been owned by John Adams Leisure Limited. Lois Allan died at her home in Farnham Common in 1989.

Hornby Trains – on the right track since 1920

There can be no doubt that Frank Hornby was one of the giants of the British toy industry, a hardworking genius who was responsible for three of the best-loved toy brands of all time: Hornby Trains, Dinky and Meccano. Since Dinky is no more and

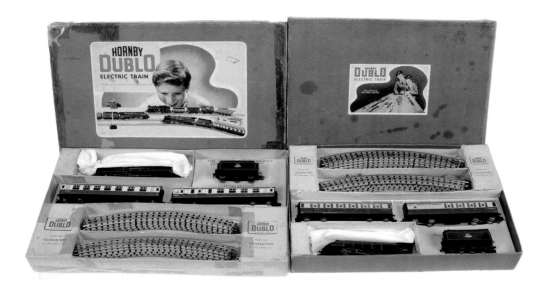

Meccano has its own entry later in the chapter, the focus here is on those marvellous model trains.

Born in 1863, Hornby was the son of a Liverpool wholesaler. Leaving school at 16, he worked for his father as a cashier before taking a job as a bookkeeper with a meat importer called David Elliott. By this time he was a married man with three children, two boys and a girl.

Having invented Meccano (see separate entry) in 1907, after the First World War Hornby introduced '0' gauge pressed metal railway engines which came in kit form and were powered by clockwork. When they proved popular, kits for further engines and accessories were introduced. By 1925 all the railway products were sold fully assembled and that same year the first Hornby electric train made its debut.

When Frank Hornby died from a heart condition in 1936 the company he had founded continued to innovate under the chairmanship of his oldest son, Roland. Introduced in 1938, Hornby Dublo was half the size of the '0' gauge system and had engines made from cast metal rather than pressed. Following a break in production during the Second World War, Hornby returned without its clockwork range and fairly soon encountered stiff competition from other companies. In 1964 the firm was

Did you know ... ?

Frank Hornby served as a Conservative MP for Everton between 1931 and 1935.

acquired by Lines Brothers, another leading British toy maker, and Tri-ang Hornby was formed. The brand went on to experience a number of upheavals but latterly the situation appears to have stabilised, allowing the much-loved brand to retain its position as the UK's pre-eminent model railway maker.

LEGO – playing well since 1932

For a small country (population-wise), Denmark packs a powerful punch when it comes to producing child-friendly names with global appeal. Written in the nineteenth century, today the fairy tales of Hans Christian Andersen are still remembered and loved worldwide. Yet Andersen's fame is dwarfed by that of LEGO, a toy developed in the twentieth century by fellow Dane Ole Kirk Kristiansen.

Dubbed 'Toy of the Century' at the turn of the millennium by *Fortune* magazine and the British Association of Toy Retailers, LEGO as we know it today first appeared in 1958 although the LEGO name originated in 1932. That's when Kristiansen, a recession-hit master carpenter and joiner with a workshop in Billund in Central Jutland, switched from house construction to smaller products such as ironing boards and stepladders in an attempt to keep his business afloat. When his customers showed a preference for the miniature products made as sales samples, Kristiansen began to make a range of toys, realising that the toy market was withstanding the slump better than other sectors. Searching for a name for his toys he combined the Danish words '*leg*' and '*godt*' – meaning 'play well' – and came up with LEGO. By 1936 the company was producing a range of forty-two distinct playthings including a wooden duck and a construction toy, as well as a number of household items.

Toy production continued during Germany's occupation of Denmark in the Second World War, halting only temporarily when the factory was destroyed by fire in 1942. Two major changes happened once the war was over: production of anything other than toys ceased, and Kristiansen and his son Godtfred invested in an expensive injection-moulding machine with a view to creating plastic toys. Automatic Binding Bricks, a LEGO brick prototype not dissimilar to a toy produced by the British Kiddicraft company, was introduced to the Danish market in 1949. After a great deal of development in the Fifties, during which Automatic Binding Bricks were renamed LEGO Bricks, the familiar stud and tube coupling system which locks bricks together was introduced in 1958, the same year that Ole Kirk Kristiansen died. It is a testament to the durability of the design that modern LEGO bricks can be used with those from 1958.

Today one of biggest toy manufacturers in the world, the LEGO Group employs over 10,000 people and is still privately owned, with founder Ole Kirk Kristiansen's grandson Kjeld Kirk Kristiansen currently in charge. In recent years the brand has branched out into different areas of commerce, with ninety-two LEGO shops worldwide, LEGO computer games and LEGO books, not forgetting 2014's highly successful *LEGO Movie*. The company gives back to the community via The LEGO Foundation which was established in 1986 to help children develop their intellectual, emotional, social and creative skills through play. LEGO has also pledged that 100 per cent of its energy will be balanced by renewable energy sources by 2020.

Did you know ... ?

A column created from all the LEGO bricks that were produced in 2012 would stretch as far as the Moon.

Meccano – mechanics made fun since 1907

It was fatherhood that put Frank Hornby (see Hornby, above) on the path to success as a toy manufacturer. To entertain his children, he constructed a toy crane using perforated strips of metal which he fixed in place with nuts and bolts. Once taken apart, the toy could be re-made in a different form. So sure was he that he had created something special, in 1901 Hornby patented his invention, using £5 borrowed from David Elliott, his employer, to pay the patent fee. An astute man who grasped the brilliance of Hornby's concept, Elliott gave him the financial backing he needed to develop it as a toy for the mass market.

With Elliott's support, Hornby launched his Mechanics Made Easy in 1902. Priced at 7s 6d, the sets contained just sixteen different components and came with instructions for making twelve distinct models. Versatile, educational and entertaining, the toys won the approval of the Head of Engineering at Liverpool University. Despite this, sales were modest for the first few years but by 1906 the venture recorded a small profit for the first time. Two significant events occurred the following

year; Frank Hornby began manufacturing the components for his construction kits and the Meccano trade name was registered. In 1908, the year Meccano Ltd was created, Elliott and Hornby parted company, leaving Hornby as sole proprietor. Home sales increased and by 1912 Meccano was being exported to a number of countries; at its peak, Meccano was manufactured in Argentina, France, Germany, Spain and the USA as well as in Britain. A publication called Meccano Monthly was launched in 1916, followed in 1930 by the formation of the Meccano Guild. Today the Meccano brand is owned by the Canadian-owned Spin Master Inc.

Merrythought – handmade huggables since 1930

While not necessarily a brand that commands universal recognition, Merrythought deserves inclusion in this book for being pretty much all that remains of a once flourishing British soft toy industry. Based in historic Ironbridge, the firm was founded in 1930 by Gordon Holmes, co-owner of a Yorkshire-based wool business, as a way to make use of his woven mohair plush which was struggling to find a market in the troubled economy. Lacking experience in the soft toy industry, Holmes persuaded Clifton Rendle, factory manager at the vastly successful Chad Valley Wrekin Toy Works, to come and run his new venture. With Rendle came several experienced workers including Florence Attwood, a brilliant designer whose products set Merrythought apart from lesser competitors. Another significant employee was Henry Janisch who left J. K. Farnell – at the time the Rolls-Royce of the UK soft toy scene – to head up Merrythought's sales force.

Published in 1931, Merrythought's first catalogue offered thirty-three different soft toy designs including no fewer than fourteen dogs plus a selection of rabbits, lambs, ducks and dogs. There were also two teddy bear lines, one priced for the luxury end of the market and the other aimed at the less well off. Subsequent catalogues introduced an increasing number of quality toys which won admirers all over the world. Perhaps the most famous Merrythought design is the Cheeky Bear which was launched in 1957 and remains a bestseller today. With cartoonish features including comically large ears containing bells, Cheeky is said to owe his name to the late Queen Mother; having examined him at a trade show, legend has it that she declared him 'a cheeky little bear'.

While most of their British soft toy rivals were seen off in the 1970s by cheap Far Eastern imports, Merrythought survived by creating imaginative limited editions for the collectors' market while continuing to produce traditional toys of high quality for a small but dedicated customer base. However, owing to a number of factors the firm went into voluntary liquidation in 2006, only to re-emerge in a much reduced capacity in the spring of 2007. Now run by Sarah and Hannah Holmes, great-granddaughters of founder Gordon Holmes, Merrythought continues to produce fine British-made teddy bears and soft toys.

Did you know ... ?

Merrythought is an old-fashioned name for a wishbone, the forked bone lying between the breast and neck of a chicken or other fowl; since Roman times it has been associated with good fortune.

Monopoly – on top of its game since 1935

In 1904 Elizabeth Magie, a 38-year-old stenographer working in Washington DC, patented a game she had spent years creating. Called 'The Landlord's Game', it was a political statement intended, in the words of its creator, as 'a practical demonstration of the present system of land-grabbing with all its usual outcomes and consequences'. Magie made up two sets of rules for her game; in the first, all players benefited from the creation of wealth but in the second, players competed to create powerful monopolies, stamping out opposition along the way. Published by a small firm called the Economic Game Company, it acquired a following on college campuses and amongst left-wing intellectuals but made little impact on the general public.

During the Twenties and early Thirties a version of Magie's blueprint became popular with the Quaker community in Atlantic City; they modified it by naming the properties on the game's board after streets in Atlantic City and giving each one a fixed price. Having played a de-politicised variant of the game while visiting Atlantic City, a businessman called Charles Todd took it back to Philadelphia where he introduced it to his unemployed neighbour, Charles Darrow. Strapped for cash and recognising the game's potential, Darrow began making and selling his own modified version of the game which he called Monopoly. His big break came in 1934 when Philadelphia's major department store agreed to stock it for Christmas. When sales proved good, other shops followed suit and Darrow found himself with such a hit on his hands that word reached the ears of games giants Parker Brothers.

Having acquired the rights to Monopoly from Darrow, Parker Brothers launched the game in 1935. The following year Waddingtons of Leeds acquired the UK rights from Parker Brothers and produced their own version featuring London streets. Other foreign variants soon followed. Owned today by Hasbro, the brand has 160 licensees worldwide. In addition to the regional variations, countless franchise tie-ins have been produced including *Doctor Who*, *Star Wars*, *Game of Thrones* and *Thunderbirds*. There is also a Monopoly World Championship which in 2015 was won by Nicoló Falcone from Italy.

Plasticine – taking shape since 1897

Non-toxic, colourful, easy to manipulate and resistant to drying out, Plasticine is the perfect craft product for young children yet it was invented with adults in mind. It was created in 1897 by William Harbutt who was born in North Shields, studied art in London and set up his own art academy in Bath in 1877. Over time he became aware of the need for a new kind of modelling clay that would allow his sculpture students to make adjustments to their work. Setting up a makeshift laboratory in the basement of his house in Alfred Street, Bath he experimented with various substances until in 1897 he hit on a winning formula that contained, amongst other ingredients, calcium carbonate, petroleum jelly and stearic acid. He patented his invention as Plasticine in 1899 and embarked on commercial production the following year, operating from an old flour mill located in the nearby village of Bathampton.

Originally available only in grey, Harbutt's Plasticine was produced in all the colours of the rainbow once its possibilities on the toy market became apparent. The company flourished for several decades thanks, during the early years, to the efforts of William Harbutt who travelled the world promoting his creation. It was on one such trip to New York in 1921 that he contracted pneumonia and died. Harbutt's Plasticine

Did you know ... ?

Wallace and Gromit, the Oscar-winning creations of film-maker Nick Park, are made from Plasticine.

remained a family concern until financial difficulties led to its acquisition in 1976 by Berwick-Timpo Ltd. When Berwick-Timpo was acquired by Peter Pan Playthings, production moved from Bathampton to Peterborough. Ownership of the brand has changed several times since then; at the time of writing Plasticine belongs to Flair Leisure and is made in Thailand.

Scalextric – racing ahead since 1957

Hard to pronounce but easy to love, Scalextric has been with us since 1957 when creator Freddie Francis launched it at the Harrogate Toy Fair. A toolmaker by trade, after the Second World War Francis founded a toy company called Minimodels Ltd in north London. In the early years Minimodels produced tinplate clockwork toys, all painstakingly designed and tooled by Francis himself. The first step towards greater things came in 1952 with the introduction of Scalex, a new clockwork range incorporating a keyless 'pull back and go' mechanism. For a few years sales of Scalex were high but as they began to slow down, Francis turned his attention to battery-powered cars. Issued in 1957, the first Scalextric set comprised two electric Scalex cars and a clip-together track with a slot running through the middle, through which the cars were guided. Although far from cheap – early sets cost over £5, then a considerable amount to spend on a toy – the new brand was an immediate success.

In 1958 Francis sold Scalextric to Lines Brothers, makers of Tri-ang Toys. Under their ownership, plastic-bodied vehicles were introduced which had the advantage of being lighter, faster and cheaper to produce than tinplate. This, together with other technical advances including variable speed controls and track improvements, brought Scalextric devoted fans all over the world, many of whom were fathers bonding with their sons as they competed to be the fastest on the track. Even Formula One legend Stirling Moss owned a Scalextric set.

Part of Hornby Hobbies since 1982, Scalextric has kept abreast of modern technological developments, most notably with the introduction of Scalextric Digital in 2004. Freddie Francis died from cancer in 1998, aged 78. In 2013 his widow Diane gave her young grandsons a pristine 1957 Scalextric set which their grandfather had put aside for the enjoyment of future generations.

Steiff – only the best since 1880

Despite attempts by other countries to claim it as their own, there is no doubt that the teddy bear originated in Germany. More specifically, the very first was produced in 1902 by Margarete Steiff GmbH, a family firm located in the small town of Giengen in southern Germany. (The 'teddy' name came later, after the toy became linked to US President Theodore 'Teddy' Roosevelt following his widely-reported refusal to shoot a bear cub whilst on a hunting trip.) At the time of their new toy's launch, Steiff referred to it as PB55 with the P standing for plush, the B for *Beweglich* (German for movable), and the 55 referencing the bear's height in centimetres.

PB55 was designed by Richard Steiff, favourite nephew of the remarkable Margarete Steiff, who had founded her successful soft toy factory in 1880 despite being confined by polio to a wheelchair since early childhood. In 1892, the company produced its first catalogue featuring the motto, 'Only the best is good enough for our children'. Simple and to the point, it is still used by the Steiff company today. By the start of the twentieth century the company had already earned an international reputation for the excellence of its products but the arrival of the teddy bear was to secure its longevity.

At first, though, it seemed that PB55 might be destined for obscurity; initial interest was modest and to cap it all Richard Steiff himself was unhappy with the string joints which enabled his bear to move its limbs. Aware that string would perish over time, Steiff experimented with metal rods before devising a system that used cotter pins and hardboard discs. When he presented his Aunt Margarete with his perfected bear in 1905, she was so pleased she immediately dubbed it '*Bärle*' which means 'little bear' and is used as a term of endearment. The world echoed her approval; demand for it was so high that nearly one million were produced in 1907 alone.

Margarete Steiff died just two years later but her company continued to flourish in the capable hands of her nephews and, later, their descendants. Their combined vision and business acumen enabled the company to grow and to weather the worst that the troubled twentieth century had to offer. Today Steiff produces an extensive selection of traditional teddy bears and soft toys as well as an imaginative range of limited editions intended for the collectors' market. Giengen now boasts the World of Steiff, a purpose-built attraction that tells the story of Steiff, and visitors can even tour the factory to see how these world famous teddy bears are made.

Did you know ... ?

Steiff's famous trademark, the *'knopf im ohr'* (button in ear), was introduced in 1904 by Franz Steiff, another of Margarete's nephews, as a way of assuring customers that they were buying a genuine Steiff article.

Subbuteo – in a league of its own since 1947

When a young man from Kent called Peter Adolph came out of the RAF at the end of the Second World War, he applied himself to inventing a game that reflected his love of football. He was aware of a tabletop football game called NewFooty which had been around since 1920 and had failed to make much of an impact, largely because the heavy lead bases of the lacquered cardboard players impeded effective flicking. Taking the basic principle of NewFooty, Adolph adapted a few elements and then designed an improved figure using a washer and a button filched from his mother's coat. Before putting his game into production, Adolph decided it would be wise to test the market; in August 1946, therefore, he placed an ad for the as-yet unmade game and then set off to the USA on a business trip. Whilst away, he received a telegram from his mother, informing him that orders totalling around £4,000 had been received from people who were very excited about the game.

Encouraged by the positive response, in 1947 Adolph patented Subbuteo and began production at premises in Langton Green, near Tunbridge Wells. When his original plan to call the game 'The Hobby' was vetoed by the Patents Office on the grounds that it was too generic for a trademark, he used his knowledge of ornithology to come up with a clever alternative, *'Falco Subbuteo'* being the Latin name for a small falcon commonly known as the hobby hawk.

The first sets, called Assembly Outfits, comprised wire goals with paper nets, a ball made from cellulose acetate, and two sets of cardboard figures with bases made from weighted-down buttons. A pitch was not included but an old army blanket was suggested as a suitable playing surface, on which lines could be drawn in chalk. By 1950 it was apparent that Adolph had a significant hit on his hands and as his success continued, he was able to give employment to hundreds of people in the Langton Green area, many of whom painted the footballer figures at home. In 1961 the first

three-dimensional plastic players were introduced, followed in 1967 by the classic heavyweight figures which are still in use today.

In 1970 Peter Adolph sold Subbuteo to Waddingtons for £250,000, staying on initially as Managing Director but leaving when he found corporate life not to his taste. In 1982 production of Subbuteo moved from Kent to Leeds, and in 1994 – the same year that Adolph died – Waddingtons were acquired by Hasbro. Although Hasbro stopped manufacturing the game in 2000, it is still produced under licence by various other companies. Today the game has a devoted international following and even holds its own World Cup in which more than thirty countries compete.

Did you know ... ?

Peter Adolph's son Mark was prohibited from playing in his school's Subbuteo league because he was too good.

Gone but not forgotten: Tri-ang
One of the best-known names in the British toy industry, Tri-ang was owned by Lines Bros, an established company with roots stretching back to the nineteenth century. Amongst many other products, Tri-ang were famous for their trains, dolls' houses, model ships and toy vehicles.

Honourable mention #1: Rubik's Cube
The Rubik's Cube was invented in 1974 by Hungarian architect Erno Rubik; produced on a modest scale in Hungary in 1977, it went international in 1980 and since then around 350 million Rubik's Cubes have been bought.

Honourable mention #2: Space Hopper
The inflatable orange riding ball with smiling face and horn-shaped handles was brought to the UK in the late Sixties by Mettoy; a blue version was also made but it wasn't as popular as the orange one. Space hoppers are still available today but they now come in a variety of sizes and colours.

Chapter 10

Travel and Recreation

A sk anyone to name a famous brand name and there's a strong likelihood that their answer will be a consumable product, probably food-related. In a straw poll conducted on Facebook, I asked people to name the first three brand names that popped into their heads. The results were illuminating, with a whopping 83 per cent naming at least one brand that falls under the consumables category. Of these, 98 per cent mentioned one or more food and drink brands while the other 2 per cent chose products that can be classified as non-edible household essentials. Just 17 per cent of respondents named at least one durable item, i.e. a product that is purchased infrequently, such as a computer or vacuum cleaner. Even more tellingly, a miserly 7 per cent of those who answered gave a brand associated with holidays, hobbies or leisure activities.

Using this admittedly unscientific data, it would be tempting to draw the conclusion that branded products are associated with the mundane necessities of everyday life (planning meals, doing the laundry, housework) while our precious free time is given over to activities untainted by the commercial world. Perhaps that is how we would like things to be in an ideal world yet the reality is that even in our spare time, brand names are a dominating presence in our lives – from the vacations we take, to the newspapers and magazines we subscribe to and the hobbies and pastimes we pursue. And maybe that's no bad thing; after all, not everyone wants to design their holiday from scratch and fewer still would choose to navigate their way around an unfamiliar city without a guidebook. So in this chapter we celebrate the brands that sit quietly on the sidelines of our lives; those that are content, metaphorically, to twiddle their thumbs while the everyday consumables occupy the limelight but spring into action when we need a bit of extra help in getting the most from our leisure time.

A-Z Guides – leading the way since 1935

Before the age of satellite navigation and Smartphone apps, losing one's way in a strange city was all too easy. Sometimes it didn't even help if the city was familiar, as London-born artist Phyllis Pearsall discovered in 1935 when she became hopelessly lost in her

home city. From this unpleasant experience, Pearsall conceived a project that was to earn her the nickname Mrs A-Z. Of course it helped that map-making was in Pearsall's genes, as was a gift for drawing and painting. She was born in East Dulwich in 1906, the daughter of a Hungarian immigrant called Alexander Gross who founded a cartographic company called Geographia Ltd. Educated at Roedean, she subsequently experienced a few tough years following the collapse of her parents' marriage. During this time she scratched a living in France, even sleeping rough when funds were at their lowest. In 1926 she came back to England where she met and married the artist Richard Pearsall. By 1935 the marriage was over and Pearsall was back in London, living in a bedsit near Victoria Station.

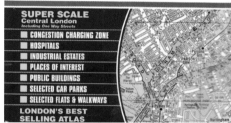

It was around this time that she lost her way one night en route to a party. Afterwards, aware that the most up to date map of London was already 17 years old, she set out to rectify the situation. Sketchbook in hand, she began tramping the London pavements until she had covered 3,000 miles and charted 23,000 streets. When her monumental task was finally complete, Pearsall attempted to find a publisher for her A-Z Atlas of London but when this proved difficult, she made the decision to self-publish with help from her father. Her commitment to the project is evidenced by the fact that she ordered a staggering 10,000 copies of the A-Z. The next hurdle was finding stockists for the guide. Hatchards, Selfridges and Foyles rejected it but her luck changed when WH Smith placed a tentative offer for 250 copies; these, according to legend, Pearsall delivered in a wheelbarrow. When the initial copies sold well, further orders were placed and before long the book could be purchased from newsstands at all the city's main railway stations. Other retailers took note and so within a couple of years, anyone needing to find their way about the capital owned a London A-Z.

Progress stalled during the Second World War when fears of a German invasion led to the prohibition of map sales. Afterwards, paper shortages meant that copies had to be printed overseas until the 1960s. By then, Oxford, Manchester and Birmingham all had their own versions of the A-Z and many more were to follow. The Geographers'

Map Trust was formed by Pearsall in 1966 in order to preserve the structure of the company after her death. Based today in Sevenoaks, the company employs forty people and produces more than 300 distinct publications including street atlases, visitor guides, road atlases and walking guides as well as city and town A-Zs. Keeping pace with technological developments, it has diversified into digital mapping and Smartphone apps but still recognises that there is a place for a printed A-Z, not least because it is an essential tool for drivers studying for 'The Knowledge', the notoriously tough test they need to pass in order to obtain a London black cab licence.

Phyllis Pearsall was awarded the MBE in 1989. She died from cancer in August 1996, having never remarried. In the interests of fairness it should be added that her half-brother, Alexander Gross, challenges Pearsall's version of events, claiming that their father was the primary author of that first London A-Z.

Did you know ... ?

Phyllis Pearsall was the subject of a 2014 stage musical entitled *The A-Z of Mrs P*. Written by Gwyneth Herbert and Diane Samuels, it achieved mixed reviews and ran from 21 February to 29 March at the Southwark Playhouse.

Automobile Association – the motorists' friend since 1905

Those that regularly experience the horror of motorway tailbacks on their daily commute might snort at the concept of motoring for pleasure but things were very different in 1905 when the Automobile Association was founded. At the time, driving was a novelty enjoyed by a fortunate few and the biggest impediment to motorists' pleasure was the perceived antagonism of the authorities. With a speed limit of 20mph on the public highway, enthusiastic drivers regularly fell foul of speed traps.

In a bid to fight back, in June 1905 a group of concerned individuals came together at the Lyons Trocadero Restaurant in London. Led by Charles Jarrott, they formed a group called the Motorists' Mutual Association but one week later the name was changed to the Automobile Association. Their first move was to recruit four non-uniformed individuals – one motorcyclist and three men on bicycles – whose job it was to scout the major roads in order to warn members of police traps. From these rather humble beginnings, the AA grew to become one of the most powerful motoring organisations in the world.

At its inception in 1905, the AA had just 100 members; by 1914 that number had reached 83,000. Patrolmen started wearing uniforms in 1909 and by 1912 they were patrolling nationwide, their brief to alert members to dangers on the road and to assist those that had broken down. As membership numbers increased, the AA expanded its interests into new areas that were connected, either directly or indirectly, with motoring. In 1907, for example, the organisation offered its first insurance policy thanks to an arrangement with Lloyd's. Repairers, hotel inspections, carefully compiled route guides and filling stations all followed in due course. In 1961 AA motorcycles were replaced by minivans and six years later the organisation phased out the vehicle badges which had been given to members since 1906. They now frequently appear on the collectables market.

As of October 2014, the AA had a personal membership of 3.92 million.

Did you know ... ?

Between 1910 and the 1960s, the failure of an AA patrolman to salute a passing member was a coded message that he was about to encounter a speed trap. At all other times the patrolman was required to salute a member displaying an AA badge on his vehicle.

Baedeker Guides – guiding our travels since 1832

There was a time not so long ago when no intrepid traveller would dream of setting forth to explore foreign climes without a copy of the relevant Baedeker handbook tucked into a pocket or valise. Karl Baedeker, the company's founder, was born in Essen, then part of Prussia, in 1801. After studying at Heidelberg University he undertook military service before gaining experience with a Berlin bookseller; his career path was almost inevitable given that his family had been associated with the publishing business for generations. In 1827 he moved to Koblenz where he established his own publishing concern and in 1832 he issued his first travel book, a careful in-depth guide to the Rhine.

When Karl Baedeker died in 1859 his three sons – Ernst, Karl and Fritz – continued with his work. The first English language guidebooks published in 1861 impressed

British and American travellers with their precise prose and meticulous accuracy. Soon their fame had spread to such an extent that the Baedeker name was synonymous with travel guides. In 1872 the company moved from Koblenz to Leipzig. Three years later they published a Palestine and Syria guide which is considered by many to be their best offering: T. E. Lawrence (of Arabia) carried a copy with him when he journeyed through the area in 1909 and 1911.

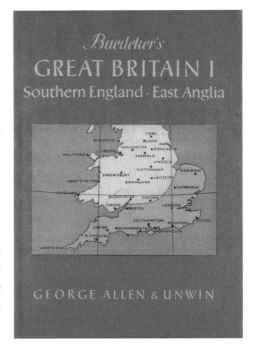

At the turn of the twentieth century Baedeker was riding high but there were stormy times ahead. Having suffered great setbacks during the First World War, the business gradually recovered but when the headquarters and archives were destroyed by Allied bombers during the Second World War, it looked as if the Baedeker story had come to an end. In Britain, the name had been sullied by the infamous Baedeker bombing raids of 1942 when the Luftwaffe had used the guides to target sites of special historic significance. Despite all this, the firm managed to resume publication under Karl Friedrich Baedeker, the great-grandson of the founder. Today the brand is owned by Mairdumont, the market leader for travel information in Germany and Europe. Modern guides are published in full colour and feature 3D laminated cut-outs showing key sights. They also include large, fully indexed maps. Old Baedekers, meanwhile, are becoming increasingly collectable with prices ranging from around £10 to several hundred pounds depending on condition and rarity.

Butlin's – family fun since 1936

Before Billy Butlin came along, a relaxing, fun-filled family holiday was beyond the reach of most working people. Born in South Africa in 1899, William Butlin (commonly known as Billy) was the son of a country gent and a travelling showman's daughter. After a peripatetic childhood in England, South Africa and Canada, he had a spell in the Canadian army before coming to Liverpool in 1921 with £5 in his pocket, a head for business head and a flair for pleasing people.

BUTLIN'S SKEGNESS
Outdoor Heated Pool and Fountain

Butlin began his career touring the West Country with a hoop-la stall. From this humble start, using a combination of hard work and natural charm, he established a small chain of amusement parks and zoos. The idea for a holiday camp came during a disappointing weekend on Barry Island; the dismal weather put paid to outdoor activities but staying indoors wasn't an option since the boarding houses expected their guests to make themselves scarce after breakfast. The experience taught him that there was a market for a holiday provider offering activities and entertainment whatever the weather, with comfortable accommodation from which guests could come and go at will.

To make his vision a reality, in 1928 Billy brought dodgem cars to the Lincolnshire seaside town of Skegness, the place he had earmarked for his first holiday camp. Within a few years he had made enough money to build his dream and so in 1936 Butlin's Skegness opened its doors to an enchanted, if occasionally windblown, clientele. Offering clean and comfortable accommodation, a breathtaking range of activities, four meals a day and evening entertainment, the camp was like nothing the British public had seen before.

Today the famous Redcoats are an integral part of the Butlin's holiday experience but during that first week in 1936, they were introduced in a bid to prevent guests from keeping themselves to themselves in the age-old British tradition. Butlin sent his cheeriest staff member on stage to tell a few jokes and then, once the guests were laughing, to make them shake hands with each other. When the experiment proved successful, Butlin kitted out nine personable young staff members in bright red blazers and set them to work keeping his guests entertained.

In 1938 the opening of a second camp, at Clacton-on-Sea in Essex coincided with the passing of the Holidays with Pay Act for which Butlin had lobbied. The slogan for the new camp, 'A week's holiday for a week's wages', reflected the fact that for the first time a holiday was within the grasp of all working people. Before he could open further camps, however, the war intervened. With holidays on hold for the duration, the Skegness and Clacton camps were requisitioned by the armed forces and Butlin was even asked to prepare a further three sites for their occupation. After the war, however, further resorts were opened at Ayr, Barry Island, Bognor Regis, Filey, Minehead, Mosney and Pwllheli.

Aware of the power of celebrity, Butlin had always courted famous friends and taken pains to book the big names of the day to perform at his camps. His extraordinary achievements were publicly recognised in 1959 when he was the subject of a *This is Your Life* television show and again in 1964 when he received a knighthood in the Queen's Birthday Honours. He died in Jersey in 1980. Butlin's is now part of Bourne Leisure, a large holiday provider that also owns Haven and Warner Leisure Hotels. The three remaining Butlin's resorts, Skegness, Minehead and Bognor Regis attract over 1.5 million guests annually, many of whom return year after year.

Hoseasons – holidays ahoy since 1944

The UK's leading provider of self-catering holidays, Hoseasons was founded in 1944 by former Lowestoft harbourmaster Wally B. Hoseason. (The fact that Hoseason is a surname rather than a contraction of the words holiday and season may come as a surprise to some people, as it certainly did to the author.) Recognising a good business opportunity, Mr Hoseason acquired a boatyard at Oulton Broad and began hiring out cabin cruisers to holidaymakers eager to explore the Norfolk Broads. When Hoseason died of tuberculosis in 1950, his son James took control of the business. Under his leadership the firm

began offering rentals of riverside holiday homes and towards the end of the decade Hoseasons advertised their boating holidays on TV in the London area.

Increased demand for self-catering holidays during the Sixties saw Hoseasons offering locations throughout the country and by the dawn of the Seventies, business was brisk for their boating holidays and holiday parks, thanks in large part to a nationwide TV advertising campaign. The company stayed fresh over the next couple of decades with new ideas and innovations; in 1982, for example, they introduced boating holidays in France while in 1996 they launched Hoseasons Country Cottages which today offers 2,300 holiday properties across the country.

In 1999, the year that Hoseasons became the first UK holiday company to take direct online bookings, James Hoseason retired from the firm founded by his father, having been awarded an OBE in 1990 for services to tourism. He died in 2009, aged 82. Today part of the Wyndham Vacation Rentals group, Hoseasons offers a wide variety of self-catering holidays across the UK as well as in Holland, Germany, Austria, Spain, France, Belgium, Switzerland, Italy and Croatia.

Kodak – innovative images since 1880

Taking a photograph used to be a complicated and expensive business. As a keen amateur photographer, George Eastman became fixated on simplifying the process. Not only did he succeed in achieving this aim, he also managed to create a multinational organisation which provided employment for thousands and gave him the wherewithal to indulge in significant philanthropy.

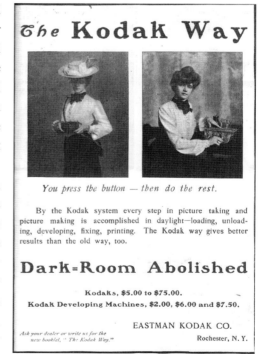

Born in New York State in 1854, Eastman went to work at 14 in order to provide for his siblings and widowed mother. His first job was as a low-paid office messenger but by 1875 he had worked his way up to the position of Junior Bookkeeper at the Rochester Savings Bank. Now earning a better wage, he was able to indulge his interest in photography by purchasing all the necessary paraphernalia and subscribing to the *British Journal of Photography*. It was an article in this publication that prompted him to begin experimenting with dry-plate photography, eventually inventing a gelatine-based dry plate formula as well as a machine for coating the dry plates.

Having patented his inventions in London in 1879, Eastman started manufacturing his dry plates the following year. Investment from businessman Henry A. Strong enabled him to leave his bank job in order to concentrate on running his company and developing further innovations in photography. In 1887, in collaboration with photography genius William Hall Walker, he invented the first camera to use paper film instead of fiddly plates. Eastman came up with the brand name Kodak, allegedly because he had a fondness for the letter K.

Problems, including quality issues with early products and the loss of key staff members, nearly halted the company in its tracks but by 1900 the situation had improved and Kodak was able to launch arguably its most famous camera, the Brownie. It went on sale priced at $1 with a roll of film costing 15 cents. As his company went from strength to strength, Eastman amassed a fortune which he was keen to share with others, donating in excess of $100 million to good causes. Sadly his health deteriorated so badly that in 1932 he committed suicide to avoid spending the remainder of his life in a wheelchair.

The company he left behind continued to innovate. In 1935 Kodachrome, the first truly successful colour film, was introduced. At first it was only available in 16mm format for motion pictures but new formats for slides and 8mm home movies became available a year later. A product with true longevity, it remained on the market until 2009 when it was discontinued due to the rising supremacy of digital photography. Ironically, for the company that in 1975 created the world's first working digital camera, Kodak struggled during the digital revolution. However, after significant reorganisation, the company has emerged as a technology company focused on imaging, providing hardware, software, consumables and services to a variety of markets.

Did you know ... ?

Paul Simon's 1972 song 'Kodachrome' was not released as a single in the UK because the BBC wouldn't give airplay to a song apparently promoting a brand name; instead, it became the 'B' side of Simon's hit, 'Take Me to the Mardi Gras'.

Ladybird – a publishing legend since 1915

A name registered by Leicestershire printers Wills & Hepworth in 1915, the first Ladybird children's books were big and thick with more line drawings than colour illustrations. It wasn't until 1940 that the books took on their familiar 56–page format of text on one side and high-quality illustrations on the other. Issued with dust jackets, they cost an affordable two shillings and sixpence, a price made possible by their relatively small size. In fact, an entire book could be produced from a sheet measuring 40in by 30in. The dust jackets disappeared in 1964 but the tempting price remained the same until 1970. A series of fiction titles featuring anthropomorphic animals appeared in the early Forties, as did some re-workings of well-known fairy tales, but it was the inspired move into educational non-fiction that really paved the way to success. Another key element was the use of leading names to write and illustrate some of the books. The result was a series of attractive books that children actually wanted to read.

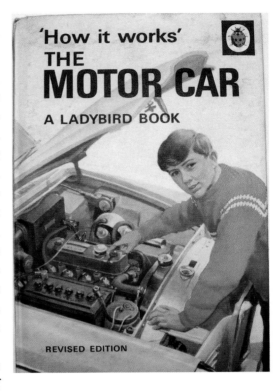

Another step on the path to success came in 1964 with the launch of Ladybird's Key Words Reading Scheme. So successful has the scheme been that it remains in print today and has sold over 95 million copies. Other popular series at the time included People at Work, Learnabout, Bible Stories, Through the Ages, Junior Science, How it Works, Natural History and many more.

In 1972 Ladybird Books was acquired by the Pearson Group but the brand is owned today by Penguin. It continues to foster a love of literacy in youngsters with a product range that starts at the baby and toddler stage and continues right up to independent readers. As for vintage Ladybirds, they are now widely sought after by enthusiasts, some of whom collect for nostalgic reasons while others simply admire the clarity and colour of the illustrations.

Did you know ... ?

First published in 1965, *Ladybird's How it Works: The Motor Car* was used by Thames Valley Police as a guide in their driving school.

Ladbrokes – taking a punt since 1902

Horseracing has been a popular British pursuit since the sixteenth century and people have been placing bets on the outcome of races for a couple of hundred years at least. Yet it wasn't until the passing of the Betting and Gaming Act in 1961 that betting shops became legal (apart from a very brief spell in the mid-nineteenth century).

The origins of Ladbrokes, arguably the UK's best known betting brand, date back to 1886 when a horse trainer called Harry Schwind teamed up with a man known to posterity only as Pennington. Together Schwind and Pennington began backing horses trained by Schwind at Ladbroke Hall in Worcestershire; however, it wasn't until 1902 when a man called Arthur Bendir joined forces with them that their enterprise really took off. Not only is Bendir credited with naming the firm Ladbrokes after Ladbroke Hall, he also persuaded his partners to start 'laying' horses – that is, placing bets on horses to lose rather than win.

Setting up in premises close to the Strand, Ladbrokes started operating as bookmakers to the rich and well-connected. Bendir was particular about this point; his attitude was that if your name wasn't in Debretts, you couldn't bet at Ladbrokes. Amazingly, this view prevailed until the firm's acquisition in 1956 by Max Parker and Cyril Stein; this uncle and nephew duo immediately opened up betting at Ladbrokes to the general public.

Following the legalisation of betting shops, Ladbrokes opened their first retail premises in 1962. Simultaneously they began offering bets on areas other than horseracing. The firm was floated on the Stock Exchange in 1967 while in the 1980s the business ventured into Europe and the USA. In 1997 Ladbrokes acquired rivals Corals but when the merger was subsequently ruled uncompetitive by the Monopolies Commission, the Corals enterprise was sold off. A more successful venture was their foray into the hotel business; in 1987 the Hilton International brand was added to their existing hotel holdings and this was consolidated just over a decade later with the acquisition of the Stakis hotel operation. The new hotels were renamed Hilton, as was the parent company which became the Hilton Group comprising two separate divisions, Hilton International and Ladbroke Gaming and Betting.

As of 2015, there are in excess of 2,700 Ladbrokes shops in the UK, Ireland, Belgium and Spain. In addition, the organisation has over 800,000 active online customers. Within the UK the company gives employment to more than 13,000 people.

Did you know … ?

In 1918 or thereabouts Ladbrokes employed an aristocratic woman called Helen Vernet to handle the small bets typically made by female racegoers. Thus Vernet became the first woman licensed to practise as a bookmaker on British racecourses.

McCall Pattern Company – simplified dressmaking since 1880

In the days before women's garments were widely available from department stores and fashion boutiques, anyone wanting a new dress had two options; they could visit a dressmaker if funds permitted but if not, they had to make the garment themselves. The problem with this was that prior to 1863, home dressmaking was very much a hit-or-miss affair. Commercial patterns did exist but they came in one size, leaving the home seamstress to estimate how much they needed to reduce or enlarge the pattern. A great many ill-fitting garments were created as a result.

In 1863 a Massachusetts tailor called Ebenezer Butterick solved this problem when he created the first graded patterns which he produced in tissue paper. The success of Butterick's idea encouraged James McCall to set up his own pattern business in 1870. A Scottish tailor living in New York, McCall followed Butterick's lead in identifying the various sections of the garments by making perforated holes in the tissue paper. These patterns were supplied in envelopes printed with a sketch of the finished garment plus a few brief instructions. Three years later McCall launched a women's magazine called *The Queen*, through which he was able to promote his designs. It was a brilliant idea which sealed the success of his venture. James McCall died in 1884 but his company continued to prosper, initially with his widow at the helm. In 1896 the magazine's title became *The Queen of Fashion* and it changed again in 1902 when it became *McCall's Magazine*, the name it kept until 2001 when it was renamed *Rosie* after Rosie O'Donnell who had become its editorial director the previous year. It ceased publication in 2002.

Perhaps the McCall Pattern Company's greatest contribution to dressmaking came in 1920 when it introduced printed patterns, leaving its rivals little option but to follow suit. Further innovation was soon to follow when the company started to collaborate with leading fashion designers such as Schiaparelli, Lanvin and Patou. This trend continued into the Fifties with McCall's producing patterns of designs created by Givenchy and Pucci. In 2001 the privately-owned, worldwide McCall Pattern Company acquired long-term rivals Butterick and Vogue Patterns.

P&O Cruises – cruising to success since 1840

For many people, a luxury cruise is the ultimate holiday experience, offering the chance to visit far-flung ports of call whilst experiencing all the comforts of a five-star hotel. In Britain, P&O is one of the most trusted names in the cruising business, sharing the dual accolade of being the world's oldest surviving cruise company and the UK's biggest home-grown line. Today the company has a fleet of eight ships of varying sizes, some specialising in cruises suitable for families whilst others cater exclusively for adults. It's fair to say things have changed a bit since 1837 when founders Arthur Anderson and Brodie McGhie Willcox won a government contract to carry mail to the Iberian peninsula.

Back then, the company was called the Peninsular Steam Navigation Company, or PSNC for short. It wasn't until 1840, when it was awarded the contract to carry the Royal Mail out east, that the name was changed to the Peninsular and Oriental Steam Navigation Company. By now running a network of routes taking in the Iberian peninsula, the Mediterranean, the Black Sea and beyond, the company began offering passengers escorted tours, initially to fill up capacity on the mail ships. In 1844 the tours received a welcome publicity boost when William Makepeace Thackeray accepted a free cruise to Egypt. Recording the trip in his *Diary of a Voyage from Cornhill to Grand Cairo*, he helped advertise P&O to a broader public. In 1904 the company offered its first dedicated cruise holiday aboard the liner *Rome*, with shore excursions organised by Thomas Cook.

In 2012 P&O celebrated its 175th anniversary with a gathering of all its seven ships (*Britannia*, the eighth, did not yet exist) at Southampton, with HRH the Princess Royal in attendance. Today the company is owned by Carnival Corporations & plc, an American-British cruise company with a combined fleet of over 100 vessels across ten cruise line brands.

Did you know … ?

From 1947 to 1972 it was possible to enjoy luxurious P&O travel to Australia for just £10; the only snag was that the journey was one-way. Devised to increase the Australian population, the 'Ten Pound Pom' scheme offered heavily discounted fares to British migrants. As an inducement to stay, however, they were obliged to repay the full fare should they decide to return home within two years.

Penguin Books – quality paperbacks since 1935

It was a weekend stay with Agatha Christie in 1934 that led, indirectly at least, to the birth of Penguin Books. On his way home from the visit to his favourite author, Allen Lane – managing editor of The Bodley Head publishing house – was killing time before his train by browsing the bookstalls at Exeter St David's station. There he made the dispiriting discovery that the only books available for purchase were poorly-produced reprints of Victorian novels. Determined to rectify the situation, Lane conceived the notion of making good-quality fiction and non-fiction available in paperback. Priced at sixpence a copy, an amount most could afford, the paperbacks would be sold at station bookstalls and tobacconists as well as from traditional bookshops.

Despite a lack of enthusiasm for the venture from his fellow Bodley Head directors, Lane pushed ahead with the project. When selecting a name for the new business, he wanted something that sounded 'dignified but also flippant'. Already he had some sort of animal in mind; dolphins and porpoises were considered before being discarded in favour of Penguin. That decision made, a young artist called Edward Young headed off to London Zoo where he spent the day sketching penguins. Although Young's design has been reworked several times over the intervening years, it has lost none of its cheerful charm.

Wasting little time, Lane managed to bring the first ten Penguin paperbacks out by the summer of 1935. Included amongst them were Ernest Hemingway's *A Farewell to Arms*, Dorothy L. Sayers' *The Unpleasantness at the Bellona Club* and, fittingly considering her part in the birth of Penguin, an Agatha Christie work, *The Mysterious Affair at Styles*. Simplicity was the watchword when it came to the design of the books; there were no cover illustrations and titles were colour-coded – green for crime fiction, orange for other fiction and blue for non-fiction. Legend has it that Penguin's future was secured by the wife of the book-buyer from Woolworth's. Initially negative about the cheap new paperbacks, he placed an order for 63,500 copies when his wife responded with enthusiasm to the sample he brought home. Whatever the truth of the story, the launch was a success and within twelve months three million paperbacks had been sold.

On 1 January 1936 Lane and his two brothers set up Penguin as a separate company, leaving Bodley Head soon after. A year later the Pelican imprint of non-fiction books was introduced, again priced at sixpence a copy, and in 1940 the children's imprint, Puffin, was launched. In 1961, when Penguin became a public company, its share offer was 150 times oversubscribed, setting a new record for the London Stock exchange.

Allen Lane received a knighthood in 1952 and died in 1970. Since then there have been many changes at Penguin. Today it is part of Penguin Random House and has offices in fifteen countries.

Did you know ... ?

In 1960 Penguin was charged under the Obscene Publications Act for publishing *Lady Chatterley's Lover*, the sexually-explicit novel by D. H. Lawrence. Following the publishing house's acquittal at trial, two million copies of the book were sold within six weeks.

Raleigh Bicycles – pedal power since 1887

In 1887 a personal interest in cycling motivated Frank Bowden to buy into a small Nottingham-based bike-making firm that had been founded the previous year by Richard Woodhead, William Ellis and Paul Angois. Having made a fortune on the Hong Kong stock market, Exeter-born Bowden had lived for a time in San Francisco where he met his future wife. By 1885 he was living once more in the UK when he was advised to take up cycling for its health benefits. When he was sold a tricycle by Woodhead, Angois and Ellis, Bowden was impressed by their operation and by the enormous potential he recognised in the fledgling cycle industry. Acting decisively, he joined the business by buying out Ellis's share. Named after Raleigh Street, the firm's Nottingham address, The Raleigh Cycle Company was registered in 1889; by 1894 Woodhead and Angois had sold their shares, leaving Bowden in complete control.

With Bowden at the helm Raleigh became the world's largest bicycle manufacturer, at one point producing more than 4.2 million bicycles annually and giving employment to around 12,000 people. Bowden received a baronetcy in 1915 and died in 1921 at his Nottinghamshire home. Following his death, his son Harold took control of Raleigh. In 1960 Raleigh became TI-Raleigh after a merger with Tube Investments, a rival cycle

manufacturer. By this time making bikes aimed more at the leisure market than at commuters, Raleigh scored a hit in the Seventies with the iconic Chopper.

Ownership of Raleigh has changed several times but at the time of writing it is part of the Dutch Accell Group. Cycle production came to an end in Nottingham in 2002 although Raleigh UK has a headquarters at Eastwood in Nottinghamshire.

Did you know ... ?

Novelist Alan Sillitoe worked at Raleigh as a young man; in his debut novel, *Saturday Night and Sunday Morning*, chief protagonist Arthur Seaton works in a bicycle factory.

The Lady – a genteel read since 1885

Curiously, since a great many people may not have seen or read a single copy, it is an indisputable fact that *The Lady* is the UK's longest running weekly women's magazine. It was started in 1885 by Thomas Gibson Bowles (maternal grandfather of the famous Mitford sisters) as a journal for gentlewomen. Bowles also founded *Vanity Fair*, a weekly magazine which became famous for its caricatures of famous figures, but he sold it two years after founding *The Lady*. Based in Covent Garden, for many years *The Lady* specialised in publishing unchallenging articles on subjects that were unlikely to embarrass delicate sensibilities. However, in terms of importance the editorial content came a poor second to the magazine's classified section which was – and remains to this day – the place to advertise for domestic staff.

According to one source, in 2008 the average age of subscribers to *The Lady* was 78. Aware that this was not a particularly healthy situation, in 2009 Ben Budworth, the current publisher and great-grandson of the founder, decided to shake things up by employing Rachel Johnson, the journalist sister of Boris, as Editor. She now holds the nominal position of Editor-in-Chief but during her tenure as Editor, while she ruffled a few feathers Johnson also managed to breathe new life into the editorial pages and bring the subscriber average age down to 52. Today, with its vibrant website and reinvigorated content, *The Lady* is no longer just a thinly-disguised vehicle for advertising domestic vacancies.

The Times – thundering news since 1785

Founded in 1785 by a former Lloyd's underwriter called John Walter, *The Times* was known in its earliest incarnation as the *Daily Universal Register*. Walter's motive in starting a newspaper had nothing to do with a passion for journalism and everything to do with a desire to recoup some recent losses at Lloyd's. Having acquired the patent for a new form of typesetting called logography, he decided that publishing his own newspaper was the best way to promote it. There was an added benefit in that he could partly finance the venture from the advertising revenue generated by the paper. Before very long Walter came to the disappointing conclusion that logography was not going to make his fortune but by this time he had been bitten by the publishing bug. In 1788 he started afresh, changing the newspaper's name to *The Times* and shifting its editorial content so that it had wider appeal. Gossip and salacious stories became the order of the day.

The situation changed for the better in 1803 when Walter's son, John Walter II, took control of the paper. A marked improvement in journalistic standards together with investment in a better printing press led to daily sales of 7,000 copies by 1817. Over time the paper came to be regarded as a strong advocate of reform, independent of political affiliations and unafraid, when necessary, to speak out against the Establishment of which it was very much a part. Under the 1817 to 1841 editorship of Thomas Barnes, the paper acquired the nickname 'The Thunderer' and by 1850 daily sales had risen to 50,000.

Hitting a low ebb towards the end of the nineteenth century, the newspaper did not fully recover its reputation until the 1920s; by the 1950s it was once again regarded as a serious, quality newspaper although it wasn't until 1966 that news replaced ads on the front cover. Today *The Times* is owned by News UK, a subsidiary of Rupert Murdoch's News Corporation; currently its circulation is in excess of 390,000.

Thomas Cook – tours to remember since 1841

In 1841 a young Leicestershire cabinet-maker called Thomas Cook chartered a train to carry 570 passengers paying one shilling each from Leicester to Loughborough. A staunch adherent of the temperance movement, Cook's motive was to take the members of the Leicester Temperance Society to a rally in Loughborough. Such was the success of this initial venture that over the next three years Cook organised further trips, thereby becoming the world's first travel agent.

Thus far he had operated without thought of financial gain but this changed in 1845 when he used the experience acquired from his philanthropic ventures to organise a commercial junket to Liverpool. Priced at 15 shillings for first class and 10 shillings for second, the trip also had a 60-page handbook for which Cook had conducted meticulous research. Encouraged by his success, he devised tours venturing as far afield as Scotland and Wales, for which accommodation and food had to be provided as well as the travel.

The next logical step was to take his tours across the Channel into Europe. Once the Continent had been conquered, he became ever more ambitious, taking tourists across North American and up the Nile by the end of the 1860s. Nor was he content to leave it at that, because a world tour that visited Japan, China, Singapore, Ceylon and India was available by the first half of the 1870s. Thomas Cook died in 1892, having taken his last trip in 1888; fittingly, for a man of such strong religious principles, its destination was the Holy Land. As of 2015, Thomas Cook Group plc remains a leader in the holiday travel industry, with sales of over £8.5 billion and more than 22,000 employees located in fifteen countries.

Did you know ... ?

In 1851, Thomas Cook made it possible for in excess of 150,000 people from Yorkshire and the Midlands to visit the Great Exhibition in London.

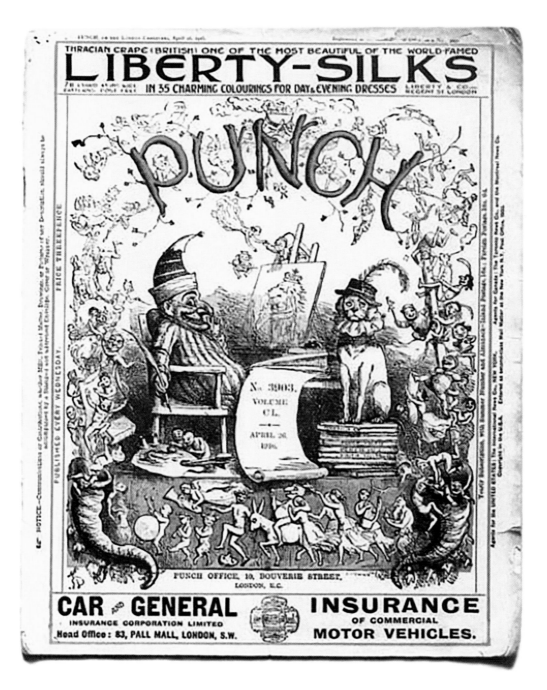

Woman's Weekly – not just knitting since 1911

When it first appeared on 4 November 1911, the cover price for this weekly publication was one penny. Latterly the magazine has become indelibly associated with women of more mature years but, according to a radio interview given by editor Diane Kenwood in 2011, its original target market was the growing number of women commuting to office jobs by train, bus and tram.

That first issue carried items about food, careers, relationships, health and beauty, topics that still make up much of the magazine's content. For many years *Woman's Weekly* has also been known and loved for its knitting patterns; many children growing up in the Fifties and Sixties wore jumpers and cardigans knitted by their mothers from patterns published in the magazine. Currently with a circulation of around 307,000, *Woman's Weekly* is published in London by Time Inc. UK.

Gone but not forgotten: Punch

Published between 1841 and 1992, Punch was a weekly satirical magazine which in its heyday featured contributions from some of our greatest writers and illustrators. Re-launched in 1996, publication stopped again in 2002.

Sources

Whilst conducting the research for this book I have trawled through countless newspaper and magazine articles, haunted manufacturers' websites, scoured blogs and special-interest forums for verifiable facts and interesting anecdotes, and traced family histories via genealogy sites. I am enormously grateful to all my sources and have endeavoured to name check them all but if by mischance one has slipped through the net, I offer my sincere apologies.

Newspapers, journals and magazines

B.M.C. Experience; *Berwick Advertiser*; *Birmingham Mail*; *Birmingham Post*; *Black Country Bugle*; *Bloomberg Business*; *Bristol Post*; *Chicago Tribune*; *Chronicle*; *Clerkenwell Post*; *Columbus Dispatch*; *Daily Express*; *Daily Mirror*; *Daily Mail*; *Daily Telegraph*; *Grocer*; *Guardian*; *History Today*; *Independent*; *Irish Examiner*; *Lincolnshire Echo*; *Live Science*; *Marketing Magazine*; *New York Times*; *Northern Echo*; *Scotsman*; *South West Business*; *Spirits Business*; *Vanity Fair*; *Wall Street Journal*.

Books and other publications

An Economic and Social History of Gambling in Britain and the USA by Roger Munting; *Don't Bet the Farm: The Encyclopaedia of Betting and Gambling* by Liam O'Brien; *Encyclopaedia of British Horseracing* by Wray Vamplew and Joyce Kay; *James May's Toy Stories* by James May; *Literature of Travel and Exploration: An Encyclopaedia* edited by Jennifer Speake; *Merrythought Teddy Bears* by Kathy Martin; *Teddy Bears* by Kathy Martin; *The Boys' Book of Airfix* by Arthur Ward; *The Liner* by Philip Dawson.

Blogs, clubs, societies etc

The Arran Alexander Collection; A Bit of History; Billy Penn; Bristol Culture; Byes of Torbay Past; Chocolate Review; Cluedofan; Cruise Critic; The Ephemera Society; The Great Idea Finder; Inherited Values; The Kitchn (*sic*); The Life of an Anglo-

American; Mental Floss; Nicole DiGiose; North East History Tour; Our Newhaven; Peter Upton's Subbuteo Tribute Website; Pyrex Love; Scotch Malt Whisky Guide; Social History Curators Group; Total Politics; Toy Tales; Typewriters.co.uk; World of Monopoly.

Other organisations

BBC; Belper Historical & Genealogical Records; British Brands Group; *Encyclopaedia Britannica*; Find My Past; Grace's Guide to British Industrial History; Heave Media; Lancaster University; New Zealand History; Ogilvy & Mather; Ohio History Central; *Oxford Dictionary of National Biography*; PBS; Phrase Finder; Spartacus Educational; Te Ara Encyclopaedia of New Zealand; Thomas Wall Trust; West Bromwich Albion Football Club.

Museums

Corning Museum of Glass; National Museums Liverpool; Thackray Medical Museum; V&A Museum of Childhood; York Museums Trust.

Product websites

A
www.theaa.com
www.addis.co.uk
www.airfix.com
www.agaliving.com
www.agbarr.co.uk
www.andrex.co.uk
www.arthurprice.com
www.az.co.uk

B
www.barbiemedia.com
www.bells.co.uk
www.brillo.com
www.butlins.com
www.butterick.mccall.com

C
www.cadbury.co.uk
www.coca-cola.co.uk
www.corgi-toys.com

D
www.dairycrest.co.uk
www.denby.co.uk
www.diageo.com
www.dyson.co.uk

G
www.gordons-gin.co.uk
www.guinness.com

H
www.harveyshalfhour.co.uk
www.hoover.co.uk
www.hoover.com

I
www.iglo.com

J
www.jacuzzi.co.uk
www.jusrol.co.uk

K
www.kenwoodworld.com
www.kodak.com

L
www.ladbrokesplc.com
www.ladybird.co.uk
www.lego.com

M
www.mairdumont.com
www.meccano.com

N
www.nestle.co.uk

P
www.parkerpen.com
www.penguin.co.uk
www.pfizer.co.uk
www.pg.com
www.philadelphia.co.uk

www.prices-candles.co.uk
www.primula.co.uk
www.princes.co.uk

R
www.radox.co.uk
www.rb.com
www.robertsradio.co.uk
www.robinsonssquash.co.uk
www.rubiks.com

S
www.saraleedesserts.com
www.savebabycham.com
www.scalextric.com
www.servis.co.uk
www.singerco.com
www.subbuteo.com

T
www.thomascookgroup.com
www.tupperwarebrands.com

U
www.unilever.com
www.unilever.co.uk

V
www.vaseline.co.uk
www.vestel.co.uk

W
http://wallsproperfood.co.uk
www.wisdomtoothbrushes.com

Acknowledgements

This book has taken a long time to research and write. It has sometimes been a lonely process but I have been fortunate in having a large pool of family members, friends and acquaintances ready and willing to lend a hand. Before thanking them, however, I must reiterate that without my many sources (listed elsewhere), this book could not have been written.

Straw poll

My thanks go to the following people for participating in the straw poll referenced in the Travel and Recreation chapter:

Carrie Attwood; Louise Bailey; Miriam Baker; Dot Bird; Sue Brotherwood; Julieann Bruce; Janet Changfoot; Maria Collin; Jackie Craig; Kim Cunninghis; Melvyn Fabb; Dave Gardner; Sue Gardner; Andrew Greetham; Gregory Gyllenship; Suzanne Hanrahan; Beatrix Harries; Elaine Hirst; Dawn James; Nick Kent; Anna Koetse; Annabel Leach; Rebecca Leach; Sarah Leach; Adam Lee; Anita Lee; Mark Lee; Olivia Lee; Richard Lee; Stephen Lee; Joanne McDonald; Steffi McIntyre; Sue McLeod; Alastair Martin; Amy Martin; Jane Martin & son; Amanda Middleditch; Graeme Miles Forbes; Michelle Mullins Nunnery; Samantha Potter; Catherine Rawcliffe; Jacqueline Revitt; Joanne Rothery; Beverley Rothwell; Elisabeth Schorr; Alice Jane Shinn; Kay Schulz; Olive Tripodi; Tracie Vallis; Monica Webb; Pauline Wood; Sally Woods; Hilary Wynn.

Images

A special mention must go to Vectis Auctions, possessors of a treasure-trove of classic toy images. I am immensely grateful to Kathy Taylor at Vectis for allowing me to use the Barbie, Corgi, Hornby, LEGO, Meccano, Scalextric and Subbuteo images found in The Toy Cupboard chapter.

Other image credits are as follows:

AGA by Rbirkby/CC-BY-2.5; Baffled doctor used courtesy of Wellcome Library, London; Beef Wellington by Jerry Pank; Bellini at Harry's Bar by Crazybobbles, London, England; Clementines by Tracy, North Brookfield, Massachusetts, USA; Collection of original Pimm's bottles by Ewan Munro; Garibaldi by James F. Carter CC-By-SA-2.5; Glass of Guinness by Kuba Bozanowski from Warsaw, Poland; M&S Penny Bazaar by Tim Green aka atouch; Jacuzzi by JimG; Pyrex and PYREX by Picofluidicist at English Wikipedia; Roberts Radio by Joe Haupt, USA; Smirnoff by Arne Hückelheim; Tarte Tatin by Djenghisj; Twinings exterior, 216 Strand by Gryffindor; Vintage Gillette Fatboy Safety Razor by Joe Haupt, USA; Vintage Singer Sewing Machine by Jorge Royan/http://www.royan.com.ar; Waldof Salad, prepared by the Waldorf Astoria, New York 2013 by Hennem08.

And finally …

My final thanks must go to Alastair, my long-suffering husband who gamely shouldered a little of the research burden when it became apparent that I would miss my deadline without his help.

Index